THE SECRETS OF
KALIS ILUSTRISIMO

Antonio Diego
Christopher Ricketts

TUTTLE PUBLISHING

BOSTON • RUTLAND, VERMONT • TOKYO

First published in the United States in 2002 by Tuttle Publishing, an imprint of Periplus Editions (HK) Ltd., with editorial offices at 153 Milk Street, Boston, Massachusetts 02109.

Library of Congress Cataloging-in-Publication

Diego, Antonio
    The secrets of kalis Ilustrisimo / Antonio Diego, Christopher Ricketts.—1st ed.
      p. cm.
    Includes bibliographical references (p.) and index.
    ISBN 0-8048-3145-9
      1. Escrima. 2. Martial arts—Philippines. I. Ricketts, Christopher, 1955- II. Title.
GV1114.38 .D54 2002
796.815—dc21   2001055648

Distributed by:

North America, Latin America, Europe
Tuttle Publishing
364 Innovation Drive
North Clarendon, VT 05759-9436
Tel: (802) 773-8930
Fax: (802) 773-6993
Email: info@tuttlepublishing.com
Web site: www.tuttlepublishing.com

Japan
Tuttle Publishing
Yaekari Building, 3rd Floor
5-4-12 Ōsaki, Shinagawa-ku, Tokyo
Japan 141-0032
Tel: (03) 5437-0171
Fax: (03) 5437-0755
Email: tuttle-sales@gol.com

Asia Pacific
Berkeley Books Pte. Ltd.
130 Joo Seng Road
#06-01/03 Olivine Building
Singapore 368357
Tel: (65) 6280-3320
Fax: (65) 6280-6290
Email: inquiries@periplus.com.sg
Web site: www.periplus.com

Indonesia
PT Java Books Indonesia
Jl. Kelapa Gading Kirana
Blok A14 No. 17
Jakarta 14240 Indonesia
Tel: (62-21) 451-5351
Fax: (62-21) 453-4987
Email: cs@javabooks.co.id

08 07 06 05 04   9 8 7 6 5 4 3 2
Printed in the United States of America

In memory of our great master, Antonio Ilustrisimo

CONTENTS

PART I
KALIS ILUSTRISIMO IN PERSPECTIVE

PART II:
FUNDAMENTALS OF PRACTICE

PART THREE

DEFENSIVE MOVEMENTS AND APPLICATIONS

Contents

Part Four

The Combative Encounter

It is an honor and great privilege to write the foreword to this book on kalis Ilustrisimo by Antonio Diego and Christopher Ricketts. They are true masters of the arts and well respected by their peers.

I began my martial arts training in 1979, and over the next eleven years I trained formally under such noted Filipino masters as Angel Cabales, Remy Presas, Herminio Biñas, and Onofre Escorpizo. Additionally, I exchanged ideas with practitioners of a half dozen other Filipino martial arts in the United States. In 1994, I made my first trip to the Philippines to research, interview, and train with over three dozen masters of the arts there.

It was in 1992 that I was first exposed to the art of kalis Ilustrisimo through Rey Galang, one of the art's senior practitioners. It wasn't until 1994 that I had the first of a dozen opportunities to date to travel to the Philippines to study this dynamic and effective fighting art. It was in Manila that I became a student of the late grandmaster Antonio Ilustrisimo and his senior masters Antonio Diego and Christopher Ricketts. It is as a result of training with these men that I immediately felt and saw a difference not only in the seriousness with which they trained and viewed their art, but also in my skill as compared to theirs. After careful deliberation, I desisted in my pursuit of the other arts and have been dedicated to the Ilustrisimo system ever since.

Although this was not an easy decision, I felt it was justified. After all, at that time I was already a certified master in Cabales serrada escrima, the appointed chief instructor of Biñas dynamic arnis, and an instructor in both cinco tero arnis and modern arnis. Moreover, I had an escrima school and seminar schedule, whereby I had been teaching and promoting practitioners in both the Cabales and Biñas systems, and had been asked by Cabales to write a book on his serrada style, which I did. I was also president of the Filipino Warrior Arts Association, which promoted these masters' respective arts in the United States. But, for me, something was still missing.

That missing link was the cultural phenomena that is the Philippines. During my trips to the Philippines I observed a different level of training in the martial art and the seriousness with which its practitioners participate in it. In the United States, even if practitioners are training hard and sweating, the art is still a hobby, a pastime. In the Philippines, even to this day, the art is looked to as a system of life-and-death survival—survival on the crime-ridden streets and survival in challenge matches offered at the hands of other seasoned arnis masters in open training forums. It is the constant threat of being challenged by other practitioners and not wanting to let your master/system down, and the daily need to deal with people trying to rob or otherwise take advantage of you, that has created a socially constructed, psychophysical training mindset. This has become a way of life wholly embraced by the arnis practitioners in the Philippines.

Mark V. Wiley in Manila with the late Antonio Ilustrisimo

It is this view of the art that has led to its continuing evolution. It evolves not so much through the masters' intellectual approach, but through practical experience and actual application. Thus, those techniques that are or become too slow or inefficient are reworked into more effective methods. Training methods, too, are created or revised to accommodate the ever-changing environment and reality of the times.

The art of kalis Ilustrisimo is at once dynamic and effective. Since the passing of the late grandmaster Antonio Ilustrisimo in 1997, the art's masters have divided into several distinct groups. This book, however, is not concerned with personal gripes or politics. It presents in a clear and easy-to-follow format the art and science of kalis Ilustrisimo as performed by Antonio Ilustrisimo and systematized over the past fifteen years by Antonio Diego, Christopher Ricketts, and Yuli Romo.

Within these pages, you will not only discover the "secrets" of a lethal and dynamic fighting art but also an artifact of Filipino martial culture, developed and honed over time and space and crafted by master swordsmen. For it is truly a sword art and not a stick art—a distinction that will elude most people because they wrongfully assume that the techniques of both are the same. I assure you, they are not.

It is with this in mind that the authors chose to present their art in both its sword and stick formats. This, coupled with their presentation of its history and fighting concepts, makes this one of the most comprehensive and in-depth instructional books on arnis available. I commend Antonio Diego and Christopher Ricketts for their efforts in perpetuating the art of kalis Ilustrisimo and offering their insights for the benefit of all.

—Mark V. Wiley

Author,

Filipino Martial Culture

Introduction

We would like to make it clear from the onset that kalis Ilustrisimo is not to be confused with kali. Kali has become the generic name used for "Filipino martial arts" as practiced in the United States. Kali is not, however, the name of an ancient, all-encompassing "mother art" of the Philippines. In fact, nobody that we know in the Philippines ever used that term, or had even heard of it, until it was used in Yambao's book *Mga Karunungan Sa Larong Arnis* and, later, in Inosanto and Johnson's book *The Filipino Martial Arts*.

Inosanto began using the term kali because his teacher, Floro Villabrille, told him it was the ancient art of our country. Villabrille also asserted that all Filipino martial arts (in addition to Chinese kuntao and Indo-Malayan silat) were phases of "kali," the art of which he was the grandmaster—asserting by inference that all other masters of eskrima, arnis, silat, kuntao, and so on, were teaching but a fraction of a "complete art" and thus had less in knowledge than he. Such an assertion has no basis in fact since the notion that Villabrille studied "kali" under a blind Moro princess in "Gindara" (Gandara), Samar is ridiculous. He did not. This is especially evident given the fact that during Villabrille's time in the Philippines, there were no longer Muslims living in central Samar, much less those of royalty; they resided in Capul Island, in northern Samar. The truth is, Floro learned his art while residing in Manila, and studied it under his uncle Antonio Ilustrisimo.

Kalis Ilustrisimo became the name of the fighting art of the late grand-master Antonio Ilustrisimo, courtesy of an American anthropologist and hoplologist named Michael Belzer, who visited him in 1985–86. The art has been in the Ilustrisimo family for more than five generations, and was simply called eskrima. However, the art of Antonio Ilustrisimo differs from the others' as a result of his instruction under Pedro Cortez, who was not a family member, and his vast personal experience in challenge matches. Therefore, while rooted in the techniques of the Ilustrisimo family art, the techniques of kalis Ilustrisimo are not necessarily the same as those practiced and taught by his well-known uncles, Regino Ilustrisimo and Guillermo Tinga, or his nephew, Floro Villabrille.

The Ilustrisimo art hails from Cebu, and is known there as olisistrisimo eskrima (an acronym of the words olisi "stick" and Ilustrisimo). After being brought to Manila, it was termed Ilustrisimo arnis. Traditionally, the art of the Ilustrisimo family was sword-based. That is, while single- and double-stick and staff-fighting techniques were practiced, they were the exception rather than the rule. The favored sword of Antonio Ilustrisimo was the *barong,* a leaf-shaped blade with exceptional balance and cutting power. The word *kalis* (as used today) is generic for "sword" and is derived from *keris (kris),* which is derived from the Turkish *kilij,* a scimitar-like sword. Kalis Ilustrisimo, then, is the sword art of Antonio Ilustrisimo.

Historically, the arts of eskrima employed both swords and sticks, while arnis was more concerned with the use of sticks. Thus, the differentiation of the terms as used by the various masters of the arts. In terms of the Ilustrisimo system, either term is correct, depending on the practitioner's focus of instruction (for example, sword or stick).

While steeped in the techniques of the sword, the groups teaching the Ilustrisimo system today are slowly moving in the direction of a stick-fighting art, in tandem with the push of Arnis Philippines to promote the arts as sport in an effort to make them more accessible and attractive to the public.

(Standing) Romy Macapagal, Doran Sordo, Benny Litonjua, Tony Diego, Topher Ricketts, Rolly Maximo, Alex Co, Alfonzo Co; (kneeling) Miguel Zubiri, Tom Dy Tang, Mark V. Wiley, Dodong Sta. Iglesia

In this volume, we have endeavored to illustrate the art in both its bladed and stick formats. In line with this, we have depicted and described each technique presented herein in three ways: single stick, single sword, and sword and dagger. We have done this in the hopes of illustrating that, while a single technique may be applicable to either a sharp or blunt weapon, there are specific variations in weapon and body positions that are necessary to make the translation effective for each weapon. Blindly exchanging a sword for a stick and performing a technique the same way is foolish and dangerous, because, for example, a stick cannot slice and a sword blade cannot be grabbed when disarming.

In consideration of the inherent space and photographic limitations of a single volume, we are able only to present an overview of the Ilustrisimo system. Thus, we do not include the fighting techniques known as *panipis, cruzada, sombrada, de cadena, sunkite, tumbada, largo mano, redonda, salok, dos andandas,* or the use of the double sticks, staff, double swords, two-handed sword, and knife. However, this book is nonetheless a significant step in introducing kalis Ilustrisimo to a larger audience and does provide the reader with a detailed historical, intellectual, and practical presentation of the art.

We wish to thank the following individuals, for without them this book would not have been possible: Thomas Dy Tang, Miguel Zubiri, and Benny Litonjua for posing for the photographs; Ronnie Ricketts, for allowing us the use of his office to shoot the photographs; Romy Macapagal, for his textual input; Yuli Romo, Rey Galang, Alex Co, and Ramon Tulfo, for their continued promotion of kalis Ilustrisimo. We especially thank Mark V. Wiley, for shooting the photographs, editing the manuscript, writing its foreword, and submitting it to the publisher on our behalf. And we thank George Donahue and Tuttle Publishing, for their interest in this project and their willingness to publish it.

PART 1

Kalis llustrisimo in Perspective

History and Development

A FAMILY ART

The instruction and perpetuation of Asian fighting arts is often characterized by family, tribal, or ethnic tradition and inheritance. That is, the arts are at once viewed as artifacts and living entities to be treasured and handed down from father to son, from chieftain to warrior, from generation to generation. The martial arts of the Philippines in general and of the Ilustrisimo family in particular are no different.

The Ilustrisimo system of eskrima is known by the name of the family that rightfully deserves the honor: "Ilustrisimo." We prefer to call it kalis Ilustrisimo, but it is also known as olistrisimo eskrima and Ilustrisimo arnis. By whatever name we call it, it still is, and ever will be, the fighting art of Antonio Ilustrisimo. In fact, as far as research indicates, the art can be traced back at least five generations in the Ilustrisimo family.

The first family member known to have practiced the art was Pablo Ilustrisimo. Of course Pablo must have had an instructor, but his name has been lost to time. Pablo is believed to have passed the art on to Juan de Dios Ilustrisimo, who concurrently passed it on to Isidro Ilustrisimo, Melicio Ilustrisimo, and Regino Ilustrisimo. Regino later immigrated to California, and was featured in Inosanto and Johnson's book, *The Filipino Martial Arts*. The head of the style at that time was Isidro Ilustrisimo, who passed the art on to Antonio Ilustrisimo, Manuel Ilustrisimo, Dalmen Ilustrisimo, and Francisco Ilustrisimo. Of this generation, the head was Antonio Ilustrisimo, who taught his nephew, Floro Villabrille, and grandnephew, Samuel Ilustrisimo. Floro later immigrated to Hawaii and was also featured in Inosanto and Johnson's book. In addition to his nephews, Antonio Ilustrisimo also taught his art to a number of non-family-members, including Antonio Diego (the current headmaster), Epifanio "Yuli" Romo, Christopher "Topher" Ricketts, Romeo Macapagal, Pedro Reyes, Ernesto Talag, the late Edgar Sulite, Rey Galang, Norman Suanico, Inocencio Glaraga, Roberto Morales, and Mark Wiley, among others.

Grandmaster Antonio Ilustrisimo, mentally prepared for all challenges

The art of kalis Ilustrisimo hails from Bantayan, an island in the Visaya region north of Cebu. In fact, Cebu has historically been known as a hotbed of *eskrimador* families, the most well known of which were the Ilustrisimos, Romos, and Saavedras. In the south was the Saavedra family, who taught such notables as Momoy Cañete of San Miguel eskrima and Filemon Caburnay of lapunti arnis de abaniko; in the center was the Romo family, who also taught Filemon Caburnay; and in the north was the Ilustrisimo family, who taught Helacrio Sulite of the Sulite style. Interestingly, Teodoro Saavedra, Pedring Romo, and Antonio Ilustrisimo were considered by their peers to be the three best eskrimadors of their time.

The Ilustrisimo family was well known and well respected among eskrimadors in the Philippines. It is interesting how many people from different places were able to train under them. For example, Melicio Ilustrisimo used to travel and teach his art. That is why you can find eskrimadors in Mindanao, Cebu, Manila, Pampanga, and Cavite all practicing the Ilustrisimo style and all having studied under the same teacher.

Not much is known of the first two generations of the Ilustrisimos. However, there are many tales of the fighting exploits of Melicio Ilustrisimo. Guillermo Tinga, the maternal uncle of Antonio Ilustrisimo, often related how Melicio used to spar with one foot nailed to the floor through a healed, scarred hole. With his seeming immobility, Melicio would lure his opponents to where he was able to employ his unique footwork, known as *lutang* (floating), wherein the mobile leg would glide back and then forward to create space to effectively lure and then counter an opponent. When employed in all eight directions, the footwork is called *walong apak* (eight steps).

Another story recounts how, while in Manila, Melicio took the challenge of an *arnisador* from Pampanga. They fought from atop a long and narrow bench. It was decided that the person who fell from the bench—or was disarmed or hit—would lose the bout. Ilustrisimo won.

Helacrio Sulite, the father of Edgar Sulite, told of how in the late 1930s to early 1940s he was able to train with Melicio Ilustrisimo after the master relocated to Masbate. During the training sessions, Melicio would sometimes lie on the ground on his back, at which time his students would encircle him and attack at random. To everyone's astonishment, Melicio would effectively disarm all of his students with his hands and feet without standing up, all the while not being hit in the process.

ANTONIO ILUSTRISIMO

Of all the Ilustrisimos, the most feared, respected, and infamous was Antonio "Tatang" Ilustrisimo. Antonio was born in Bagong, Bantayan, Cebu, in 1900. As a young boy, Antonio studied eskrima under his father, Isidro. Around the age of ten, however, Antonio became fed up with the strict training and decided to travel to the United States. In an effort to do so, he stowed away on a boat he thought was headed to America. When the boat docked soon thereafter and Antonio disembarked, he found the people of America and the place itself to be very much like that of Cebu. As it turned out, he had not reached America but Zamboanga City, Mindanao, in the southern Philippines. There he met a Muslim headed for the island of Jolo. Ilustrisimo joined him, and was taken in by a man named Hadji Muhammed. Ilustrisimo was soon after adopted by Muhammed and given the name of Montesali, eventually, becoming his favorite adopted son.

It was during his return to Zamboanga, after his exile from Jolo for a homicide, that Antonio studied arnis under master Pedro Cortez. Cortez worked as a government agent, pacifying villages so wild and remote that the Philippine Constabulary dared not enter them. Antonio recalled the style of Cortez as being similar to that of the Ilustrisimo family and consisting of the techniques found in this manual. In addition to Ilustrisimo, there were six other students training under Cortez at that time. Of the seven students, Antonio was the favorite of the master. Cortez went bandit hunting with his Muslim weapons and fought challenges with his *barong*. It was Tatang who was the one who carried the weapons for him—a distinct honor among disciples of famed eskrimadors.

One morning, a panting messenger ran up to Cortez to tell him that the warring clans in one village were drawn up in the village square ready to cut one another to pieces. Except for young Ilustrisimo, no one volunteered to go with Cortez to pacify the villagers.

Antonio "Tatang" Ilustrisimo relaxing

As they entered the village, Ilustrisimo expected the villagers to descend upon them and hack them to death. But Cortez coolly walked between the lines of drawn men and told them to lay down their swords and knives at his feet. Amazingly, the men obeyed.

Cortez told Ilustrisimo to rope the blades into a bundle. The two of them then shouldered the bundle and calmly walked out of the village. Cortez had used an *oracion* (incantation) to make the men capitulate.

When Ilustrisimo was seventeen years old, he went to drink beer in a store. As Ilustrisimo started to buy the beer, a Muslim standing nearby began to berate him, because drinking alcohol is forbidden among Muslims. When Tatang ignored him, the Muslim cursed more vehemently and advanced on Tatang, drawing his kris. As he prepared to slash at Ilustrisimo, Tatang drew his own barong and cut off the attacker's head in one motion, using a technique called *tumbada*.

Tatang in Moro garb, performing dos manos solo baston

In an effort to avoid a clan war, Muhammed paid blood money for the homicide, then loaded his adopted son with money and presents and sent him back to Bantayan. Ilustrisimo had a tearful reunion with his family, but time and experience had changed him, thus making his parents unable to identify him at first.

Tatang was soon thereafter jailed on the island of Santa Rosa for killing a man in a duel. While in jail as a living-out prisoner in charge of prisoner road gangs, Ilustrisimo met a young boy named Timoteo Maranga. Maranga's son, Rigo, relates the story of how his father would carry Tatang's weapon for him prior to engaging in his challenge matches. Interestingly, Maranga later went on to study and master the Balintawak style of arnis under that art's founder, Venancio "Anciong" Bacon.

In his attempt to research if there were any crossover techniques between the Ilustrisimo and Balintawak styles as performed by his father, Rigo Maranga accompanied Antonio Diego and Yuli Romo to the home of Tatang Ilustrisimo in Tondo, Manila. After witnessing the Ilustrisimo style firsthand, Rigo found that his father had indeed been influenced by Ilustrisimo. When asked why he didn't teach Maranga much, since, after all, the boy was his right-hand man and carried his weapon for him, Tatang explained only that there was not much time and that his art is that which kept him alive, and that the reason he was undefeated in real combat was because his style was so different from that of others. Thus, to instruct someone in his art would do much to reduce his chances of surprise when he was matched against other eskrimadors.

Tatang applies a knife defense on Tony Diego

Tatang was restless and could not stay in one place. He went from island to island in search of work. One town where he worked was terrorized by three hoodlums, the Vasquez brothers, who were so formidable that policemen walked the other way whenever they saw the trio approaching.

During the town fiesta, Tatang caught one of the brothers cheating at dice. Tatang so frightened the man that the latter dove out of the window of the house and into the swollen river below, from where he shouted that he would return to kill the master.

A few hours later, the man was back with his brothers. Although some townsfolk tried to stop him, Tatang took up a fighting *bolo* and walked out to the street where the Vasquez brothers were yelling for his head. The brothers encircled Tatang, two in front and the other behind. Tatang silently chanted his oracion as the man behind began to throw fist-sized rocks at him. But it was as if an invisible force field protected Tatang. The rocks either fell short or were deflected. The oracion proved effective.

Tatang advanced on the two brothers in front of him. He swung his bolo and, like a wet twig, the thumb of one attacker fell to the ground. As Tatang turned to the other man, the brothers fled, never to return.

In the 1940s, Ilustrisimo relocated to Manila. It was here, together with the known eskrimadors of that time, that he worked on the shipping docks in Tondo. Perhaps the most famous eskrimador working the Tondo docks with Ilustrisimo was Felicisimo Dizon, the famed instructor of Angel Cabales. Dizon was a contemporary of Melicio Ilustrisimo and Islao Romo.

Although the name of the teacher of and style practiced by Islao Romo is unknown, he was the most famous teacher in Cebu during the forties. The other well-known masters there were Teodoro Saavedra and Doring Dilaw. And although the teacher of Felicisimo Dizon is also unknown, he was known to have been, along with Agapito Ilustrisimo, a member of the original Doce Pares Society of Mt. Banahaw, Laguna. This should not be confused with the Doce Pares Association that was founded in Cebu in 1932.

It was in San Nicholas, near the waterfront, where Dizon, Ilustrisimo, and another eskrimador, named Antonio Mercado, trained together. During that time, Ilustrisimo's nephew, Floro Villabrille, came to join the group and study eskrima under his Uncle Antonio. Villabrille's "grandmaster" certificate from the Philippines, moreover, says eskrima, not kali. For whatever reason, upon immigrating to the United States, Villabrille felt a need to hide this fact and create a myth of training with a fictitious blind Moro princess named Josephina. This story, however, is sheer nonsense. In fact, upon learning of the story in Inosanto and Johnson's book, Tatang was so amused he laughed for several minutes. The blind princess story was later challenged in Wiley's books, and, it is hoped, given clarification here, so that this absurd story is finally put to rest.

Tatang applies a disarm on Christopher Ricketts

Although Dizon, Ilustrisimo, and Mercado were trained in different styles, they hung around, practiced their arts, and sparred together, thus influencing each other's style. In fact, close examination reveals that the styles of Felicisimo

Dizon (and by extension Cabales) and Antonio Ilustrisimo (and by extension Villabrille) are quite similar. The differences are to be found in each art's respective master's preferred type and length of weapon, body size (which effects footwork and movement), and experience in actual challenge matches (or lack thereof). It is as a result of these personal traits that the arts now appear to be different. Individual style not withstanding, it was said that among them Ilustrisimo was the fastest—most likely because he was taller and stronger. In addition, Tatang was a good *cucaracha* dancer, which is why the footwork of his system is said to be so fast. However, Tatang was not so much fast as perfect in his timing.

When World War II hit the Philippines, Ilustrisimo, Dizon, a man named Pedic Naba, and the other eskrimadors of their group became members of the Filipino guerrilla forces fighting the invading Japanese forces. Toward the end of the war, it was these men who became the *berdugo* (executioners) of the *makapili* (traitors). They would round up the Filipino traitors and take them to a place on Madrid Street and decapitate each of them with single blows of their bolos.

Mark Wiley and Tatang Ilustrisimo training together

After working the Tondo docks, Antonio Ilustrisimo was granted a work visa and became a merchant marine seaman. During one of his layovers in Malaysia he had a fight inside a bar against four men. There were men and lots of women drinking with Tatang because at that time he had at lot of money. A man bumped into Tatang, beginning a fistfight. Tatang was standing in front of his three drinking compadres. When the Malaysians came at them, Tatang would hit and then throw them to the three men in back of him. The men said that as the Malaysians flew through the air, they could see through their *sarong* (kiltlike waist cloth) that they had no underwear on.

During his tenure as a seaman, the reigning martial arts champion among Asian sailors was an Indonesian practitioner of pencak silat. He boasted of the many men he had killed in duels and dared anyone to fight with him.

Growing tired of his boasting, Filipino sailors called Antonio Ilustrisimo from India and offered to pay all his expenses to go to Singapore and fight the Indonesian. Ilustrisimo accepted.

It was a sweltering night when the duel took place. The Happy World Stadium was filled with a wildly betting, blood-hungry crowd that had come to watch a fight with naked blades. Perhaps one of the combatants would die.

The Indonesian was first in the ring, brandishing his long knife to roars of approval from his supporters. Then Ilustrisimo climbed into his corner and quietly watched the Indonesian. As the two warriors approached one another, the Indonesian swung his blade. Ilustrisimo angled his body and in a single motion slashed the man's wrist, thus rendering him unable to continue. After the fight, the Indonesian asked to become the student of Tatang, who declined the offer and then rejoined his ship.

On another occasion, while resting between voyages, a close friend of Tatang visited Ilustrisimo's home and appealed to him to help get rid of a troublemaker who was terrorizing the pier area. The man was an expert arnisador and had already defeated the champions of the neighborhood in territorial fights.

Tatang sent a message to the arnisador to either leave town or meet him beside the pier for a duel. The man arrived at the appointed time, swaggering and with an unsheathed knife. The arrangement was for Tatang's friend to take on the bully, with Tatang taking over in case the bully won. Tatang's friend was disarmed, at which point Tatang took over the fight. Tatang held a short lead pipe in his right hand. Tatang spread his arms like a crane and shouted, "I'm open. Hit me." As the man lunged, Tatang turned to evade the thrust, and in the same motion brought down the lead pipe on the man's head, crushing his skull with a technique called *atracada cerrada*.

Even into his senior years, Antonio Ilustrisimo was no stranger to fighting. A well-known story recalls a time when three robbers boarded a jeepney. One mugger sat with the driver in front, while the two others seated themselves at the rear entrance.

When the eighty-year-old Ilustrisimo boarded the jeepney carrying a two-foot aluminum rod, they barely glanced at him.

As the jeepney entered a dimly lighted park, the muggers pulled out their knives and ordered the passengers to hand over their wallets and jewelry. Instead of complying, Tatang swung his aluminum rod, sending the teeth of one mugger flying out of the window while simultaneously ripping the stomach of the other with his bare hand. The remaining mugger was so scared that he leaped out of the moving jeepney and fled.

On another occasion when Tatang was eighty, Christopher Ricketts and Edgar Sulite had the opportunity to see the fighting skills of their master first hand. In this instance, an eskrima student from Australia was visiting Manila. Wanting to test his skills, he challenged Sulite to a sparring match. Wishing to keep it "friendly," Sulite and the student donned headgear and used a lightly padded rattan stick. Sulite took the immediate advantage, but the Australian, being six inches taller than Sulite, kept pressing his attack—trying to overrun and sweep him. Edgar was able to stand his ground for some time, but was eventually moved off balance and fell to the ground, breaking his ankle in the process. Despite the break, Edgar opted to continue.

It was at this point that Christopher Ricketts stood up and told Edgar to rest his foot and said that he would take over the match. As Topher stood up, Tatang stopped him and said that it was he who would finish the match. In one instant, and with no headgear or body armor and despite his advanced age, Tatang grabbed Sulite's padded stick and instantly began attacking the student from Australia from head to toe. Although Ilustrisimo was also hit a few times, he pressed his attack and forced the student to the ground. He took cover under a boxing speed bag platform, pleading for an end to the match. But Ilustrisimo was in combat mode and didn't let up his barrage of strikes until his opponent dropped his weapon. Although not a life-and-death altercation, the seriousness with which Ilustrisimo defended his art and pressed his attacker was nonetheless serious and real.

Edgar Sulite and Christopher Ricketts training together

Tatang retired from his itinerant life as a seaman in 1982 but refused to teach arnis. He told Antonio "Tony" Diego, the most persistent pleader, "Young man, I learned arnis to save my life, why should I proclaim its secret to the world?" Persistence paid off, however, and the Ilustrisimo style is now being taught around the world.

ANTONIO DIEGO

Antonio Diego is currently fifty-three years old and resides in Tondo, Manila. He became interested in arnis while still a small child growing up in Pasil, Cebu. Some historians believe that Pasil was the location of the kingdom of Raja Humabon. According to historical accounts, Magellan landed in a place between a river and a small creek, and there is no place like that in Cebu except Pasil.

Grandmaster Antonio Diego

Since before World War II, Pasil was known as a place where great eskri-madors resided, practiced their craft, and fought. Among the famous masters in Pasil at the time were Islao Romo and his children, Pedring and the late Carlito. Other noted eskrimadors living there were Atty. Rodel Necasio Labuntog, Carling Cabasa, Filemon Caburnay, Timoteo Maranga, and Vicente "Intin" Carin. These men greatly influenced Diego in his perception of eskrima, because the art as practiced at that time bears little resemblance to the way in which it is practiced today. Most notably, at that time, the masters trained with swords, not sticks.

The eskrimadors of Pasil used to gather and practice at the home of Atty. Rodel because he had a large outdoor space in which to maneuver. Diego was around the age of eight or nine at the time and was fond of watching the masters and then trying, as best he could, to imitate their movements. Although he was young, the very visible cuts and gashes in the eskrimadors' hands, arms, and legs— just from training—left an indelible impression on him. One time he witnessed a practitioner training his empty-hand skills against a sharp knife, only to have the blade penetrate right through his hand as he was slightly off time. They also prac-ticed dumog (a native wrestling art) along with their eskrima. First they would train with their bolos and then move on to grappling.

Diego began his formal training in the Balintawak style of arnis under Fidel Mosqueda and later met a man named Beding, one of the students of Atty. Jose Villasin, who also shared some of his knowledge with Tony. Diego also had a friend who was a senior student in the Doce Pares Association of Cebu, who shared with Tony what he knew about the art.

Upon relocating to Manila in 1973, Diego took a job working the Manila shipping piers. It was here that Tony was introduced to two arnisadors named Santos Abijo and Fidel Mosqueda. These men were also from Pasil and knew the styles of Islao Romo and Balintawak. After work, when there were no peo-ple around, the men used to practice inside a warehouse. Tony began learning the Balintawak system from them in 1974.

During one of their practice sessions in 1975, an old man from Cebu approached Tony and told him that there was a man in Manila named Ilustrisimo who had not been defeated in combat, before or after the war. Since Ilustrisimo was considered the best, the old man suggested that Tony seek him out.

Tony found out where Ilustrisimo lived and paid him a visit. Unfortunately at that time, because Ilustrisimo was a merchant marine, he was abroad. Disappointed but not disheartened, Tony looked for another arnis teacher. He saw a sign advertising modern arnis and decided to enroll. For the next year, until Ilustrisimo returned from sea, Tony studied modern arnis under Roberto "Berting" Presas.

Upon hearing that Tatang was back in Manila, Tony dropped out of modern arnis and again went to Ilustrisimo's residence. When Diego arrived, Tatang inquired as to his purpose in being there. Diego told Ilustrisimo that he had heard about him and that he wanted to learn his style of arnis. Ilustrisimo then asked Tony where he was from. Upon hearing the town of Pasil, Tatang remarked that it was a place of great eskrimadors. Ilustrisimo then asked Diego to show him some of his eskrima movements. Tony did, after which Tatang told him, "Very good. You can fight now. Go home." To which Tony replied, "No, Manoy. I want to learn from you."

Reluctant to share his knowledge of eskrima, Ilustrisimo asked Diego to strike at him with his stick. When Tony did, Ilustrisimo countered with one swift blow, sending Tony's stick sailing through the air at great speed. The two men then sat down and talked for a while, after which Ilustrisimo told Diego to go home.

Determined, Tony kept returning to Ilustrisimo's home, day after day. The place where Tatang lived was Tondo, an area made up at that time (and much like today) mainly of makeshift shanty structures and populated with squatters. Crime and murder were rampant. Being somewhat young and inexperienced in life-and-death combat, it was dangerous for Tony to travel there. However, so legendary was Ilustrisimo's skill in Tondo that he earned the nickname

"Dagahoy," after the famous revolutionary fighter. Thus, whenever Tony faced possible trouble in Tondo, he needed only mention the name of Dagahoy, and the thugs would allow him to pass unscathed.

The next day, Tony went again to Tondo, this time accompanied by his friend Teban Salcedo, whose eskrima teacher was a student of Felicisimo Dizon. Salcedo was a small guy who played the art low to the ground and employed the *payong* (umbrella) technique to maneuver beneath an opponent's blows. Upon arrival, the two eager students presented Ilustrisimo with a gift of *pulutan* (mixed finger foods), but the old man again refused to instruct them. Tony then got the idea that they should get Tatang drunk and that if he and Salcedo began practicing their own art, Tatang would get disgusted and show them the so-called "real" art. The two began moving around the small, one-room home, but to no avail. Finally, they made some comments between themselves about the ineffectiveness of Tatang's art against their strikes. With that, the old warrior became angered, rose to his feet, stepped in the middle of the action, and threw Salcedo beneath a table along one wall. So afraid of Tatang was Salcedo that he remained under the table until Ilustrisimo cooled off.

The next day, and for several more days, Diego traveled to Ilustrisimo's place, this time with Carling Nicol, an arnisador from Iloilo. Every day they would just sit and drink alcohol, hoping to coax the old man into demonstrating his art. Finally, Tatang agreed to show them how he would counter Carling's strikes. As the man initiated his first strike toward Ilustrisimo, Tatang merely struck the *punyo* (butt end) of his stick with his open palm, sending the stick flying out of Carling's hand!

After several more rejections from Tatang, Tony learned that the old warrior was fond of *sabong* (fighting cocks). On his next visit, Tony brought Tatang a cock as a gift. Ilustrisimo still refused to take him on as a student. However, Ilustrisimo's wife told her husband that Tony seemed quite sincere and loyal and that he should reconsider the proposition. Tatang replied to her, "My system is only for myself. Nobody else knows it, and that's why I have never been defeated." But Diego kept returning. Ilustrisimo began to pity Tony, and finally took him on as his first student. This was in 1976.

The late Dr. Guillermo Lengson, the founder and president of the now-defunct Karate Arnis Federation of the Philippines, had an arnis fighter named Tadepa who traveled to Cebu for a tournament and to learn arnis from Timoteo

Diego poses with a sabong, a fighting cock

Maranga. Upon hearing that Tadepa, a Cebuana from Pasil was now living in Manila, Maranga told them that they should try to locate a great arnisador there named Antonio Ilustrisimo.

On returning to Manila, Tadepa, accompanied by Epifanio "Yuli" Romo, went to Luneta Park, across from the Manila Hotel, because there was a group of arnisadors practicing there. The style was Balintawak, and Tony Diego was among the members of the group. On hearing of the men's interest in locating Ilustrisimo, Diego remained silent. Knowing what he went through to finally get the master to take him on as a student, Diego was not about to bring these men to his master so easily.

However, one day sometime later, when Tony went to visit Ilustrisimo, he found a man bent over some coals, grilling fish for Tatang. When the man stood up, Tony saw that it was Yuli Romo! They immediately began laughing, for all this time they were talking about the old man while practicing Balintawak in the park, and neither knew the other was training with Ilustrisimo during the week. They immediately became good friends and training partners.

When teaching the two stalwarts in his small, one-room home, Tatang would stand in front of a mirror-faced cabinet, with a light bulb hanging above, and maneuver. His sense of distance and spatial relationships was so acute that he would not hit anything. The next week, Diego and Romo were practicing again, this time with their backs to the cabinet and standing under the light. They broke everything! From that day on, they always made sure that Tatang was the one with his back to the cabinet.

Like his great master, Tony Diego has also used his skills in real fights, a few of them life-and-death encounters. One such incident took place on Pier Four, where Tony works. An arnis expert from Batangas traveled north to Manila at the invitation of a friend to match his skills with the local eskrimadors. The locals taking the challenge were not beginners, but neither were they experts. To make a long story short, the Batangueño played with them and mocked their skills.

Diego happened to be on duty at the time, and somebody told him what was happening. Diego went over to the place where the matches were taking place and observed the Batangueño in action. While he was basking in his glory and enjoying his victory over the local eskrimadors, Diego asked him if he'd like to match skills. Feeling confident, the Batangueño obliged. Being more respectful than his opponent, Diego did not play with the fighter or mock his skills, as his opponent had done with the others. Diego simply made him look as if he were standing still.

Epifanio "Yuli" Romo in Moro garb, performing doble baston

Diego also had a match against an arnisador from Aclan. The fight did not last long, because Diego immediately went for the man's eyes, and he, likewise, immediately conceded defeat.

From that fateful day in 1976 when Antonio Ilustrisimo accepted Antonio Diego as his student, until the master's passing in 1997, Tony remained Tatang's most trusting and loyal student. It was in 1992, that Ilustrisimo formally named Diego as the heir apparent to his fighting art of kalis Ilustrisimo.

CHRISTOPHER RICKETTS

Christopher "Topher" Ricketts was first introduced to arnis around 1967 or 1968. Topher was practicing kung fu and karate at that time. A man from Quezon province named Edgar Cloefe, who was a practitioner of the rapillon style of arnis, was staying across the street from him. They were introduced to one another through a mutual friend—Topher as a karate expert and Cloefe as an arnis expert. After the formalities, the two were asked if they would like to spar, *nunchaku* against stick. Topher declined, feeling it was not an even match because the stick was longer than the nunchaku. One of Topher's students accepted, but was defeated by Cloefe. The meeting left an impression on Topher, so much so that he sought out Cloefe's father, Mang Sciano, for instruction in arnis. Uncomfortable with the idea of taking on a student who was already versed in another style, Sciano declined Topher's request.

It was in 1969 that Topher met Dr. Guillermo Lengson, an arnisador from Pangasinan, who was studying arnis under Remy Presas at Lengson's dental clinic in Manila. At that time, Presas had not yet developed his so-called modern arnis style and was teaching Balintawak to Lengson, who, in turn, taught Presas the double-stick art of sinawali. While there, Topher also had to chance to meet a man named Jimmy Gales, who had his own arnis style, which he called sphinx, in which he used the *centro baston* (central grip) and *susi* (inverted grip) styles of wielding a stick.

From 1973 to 1978, Dr. Lengson's Karate Arnis Federation of the Philippines sponsored full-contact weapon and empty-hand fighting tournaments, which were televised every weekend. It was on this show that Topher witnessed the impressive escrido style of Cacoy Cañete, whose demonstration was given at the intermission between bouts. However, Topher felt that the skill level of the actual arnis tournament competitors was low, because the winner was decided by the first person to land a single blow, rather than by accumulation of points. Although single stick was the popular mode for tournaments at the time, in this tournament it was espada y daga (the concurrent use of a long and short stick). At the request of Lengson, Topher and his students entered the tournament, wherein Topher and many of his students won their matches because of their well-honed timing. As a result, Topher felt that anyone with even a modicum of skill in martial arts could wear armor and swing a stick and win, and thus he lost respect for arnis.

Master Christopher Ricketts

It wasn't until 1984 that Ricketts developed a newfound respect for this native Filipino art. It was then that he met Tony Diego and Antonio Ilustrisimo through mutual friends Alex Co and Pete Reyes. Since Topher had a video camera, they asked him if he would be willing to videotape the techniques of a local *aikidoka* named Ernie Talag (who was also a student of Ilustrisimo). It was during this video session that Topher witnessed the dynamic fighting art of kalis Ilustrisimo. He immediately became a student of the old master.

It was also in 1984 that Ricketts met Edgar Sulite through Tony Diego. Although also a student of Ilustrisimo, Sulite's style of fighting was based in the de campo uno-dos-tres orihinal style of Jose Caballero and the pekiti tirsia style of Leo Gaje, Jr. It was during one of their training sessions that Edgar asked Topher to spar with him. Topher agreed after Tony urged him on. After his rounds with Edgar, Topher sparred Tony. Topher then pushed Sulite and Diego together and told the two of them to spar. Since they were both masters, they had never sparred with one another before. But this time they could not decline.

Ricketts and Sulite preparing to spar

Ricketts felt that it was quite evident at that time that Diego's skill was far superior to Sulite's. It should be understood, however, that in those days eskrimadors didn't engage in free-style sparring, for fear of seriously injuring their training partner—fighting skills were developed through two-person drills. After that incident, however, Topher was able to influence the Ilustrisimo group by helping to develop their sparring skills as he had developed his own through years of full-contact martial arts and boxing training.

Yuli Romo practicing free-flow drills with Topher

Ricketts also recalls sparring with Tatang, wherein the master struck his eyes in the first instant. "Actually," recalls Topher, "he was respectful, but I was saying to Tatang that he could not hit me. I was saying that so I could see how the old man would press his attack on me." At this, Tatang stood up and began striking Topher on the head, feinted left and then struck his right eye. "There was no control," laughs Ricketts. "He just hit me so hard in the eye that I dropped to the ground searching for it. I thought he had actually knocked it out." When

Topher stood up, Tatang asked him if he was okay. On hearing that he was, Ilustrisimo continued his barrage of strikes on his student. "An old master willing to fight to the end, even in a training session—that's how I remember Tatang," reflects Ricketts.

Since Tatang was not your typical teacher, the group would constantly get together to practice the techniques he taught. Diego, Romo, and Sulite would often bring Tatang around to Topher's home in Las Piñas to train, and Topher would videotape their sessions. It was from that time on that Antonio Ilustrisimo's fighting art began to take shape in terms of a systematic progression for teaching.

SYSTEMATIZING THE ART

In the early days when Diego and Romo were first learning from Tatang, the old master had a unique way of imparting his style to them. Every time the two of them would ask Tatang to show them a technique, he would tell them to strike at him, at which time he demonstrated his natural countermovement. The next time, his movement might be different, even though the attack seemed to be the same. It was this method of teaching that frustrated the students. When Tony and Yuli asked why he didn't repeat the same counter against the same strike, Ilustrisimo told them that their energy or the angle of their strike was slightly different than before, thus requiring a different response. Given the fact that Ilustrisimo had never learned the art in a "by-the-numbers" format, he didn't understand the value of teaching it in such a way. Thus, it was difficult for Tony and Yuli to try and learn his techniques—let alone catalogue them.

It is because of his unusual teaching method that many people have said that while Antonio Ilustrisimo was a good fighter, he was not a good teacher. But if you really analyze his method of imparting his art, you see that he was in fact a great teacher. While it is true that Tatang did not teach his art in the usual step-by-step manner, he actually taught his students something much more valuable: the experience of the techniques. In other words, he did not teach anyone how to learn his techniques, but he made others understand the techniques from the onset by giving them the true experience of their essence.

The late Antonio Ilustrisimo with the authors

However, not understanding Tatang's teaching method at the time, one day Tony and Yuli brought a psychic named Bonnie Tan—who was also a teacher at the Catholic University of the Philippines—with them to Tatang's home to try to analyze Ilustrisimo's art. Tony and Yuli then proceeded to attack Tatang in turn, who countered naturally. They then asked Bonnie what he thought. Bonnie replied that the style was too hard to analyze, that Tatang just moved and that it was random. The psychic then told them that that was the first time he had seen such types of movements, even though finding order in chaos was his specialty.

Tatang shows Diego a thing or two about sparring

It was with the aid of modern technology that kalis Ilustrisimo was finally systematized. At various times, over a period of several years, Christopher Ricketts, Edgar Sulite, or Tony Diego would bring Ilustrisimo over to Ricketts's home in San Miguel Village, Makati for training. Once there, they would take turns attacking their master while one of them observed and the other video-taped the sessions. Afterwards, they would analyze the tapes and discuss the system among themselves, focusing on what techniques were repeated against what types of attacks. From there, they were able to find the structure in Tatang's freedom. They then set about constructing a teaching syllabus and training drills to impart the art to a larger audience.

"The Masters of Arnis" in Australia, with Tony Diego (second from left),
Rey Galang, Edgar Sulite, and Christopher Ricketts (second from right)

KALIS ILUSTRISIMO TODAY

Today, the art of kalis Ilustrisimo is famous around the world for its dynamic fighting techniques and the exploits of its late grandmaster, Antonio Ilustri-simo. In fact, the art or its practitioners have been featured in the books of Inosanto and Johnson, Sulite, Wiley, and Siebert, and in such magazines as *Inside Kung-Fu, Martial Arts Legends, Journal of Asian Martial Arts, Fighting Arts International, Austral-Asian Fighting Arts, Rapid Journal, Tambuli, Phoenix,* and *Vortex*.

Rey Galang, in the tulisan knife posture

Mark V. Wiley with solo baston

Such recognition, however, was a long time coming and is well deserved. While many practitioners of various arnis styles in the Philippines and around the world have sought out the style of Antonio Ilustrisimo, the art was first brought overseas in 1985. The place was Australia, and the event was called "The Masters of Arnis" and was organized by Rey Galang, who was residing there. At that time, Rey was a student of Christopher Ricketts, and later he became a direct student of Tatang Ilustrisimo. He invited Christopher Ricketts, Tony Diego, and Edgar Sulite over to Australia for a series of seminars in Melbourne and Sydney. Thus began the kalis Ilustrisimo group in Australia, whose membership today includes Raymond Floro, John Chow, and Raneer Favis.

It was in 1986 that Christopher Ricketts visited the United States for a year and taught the art in Southern California. Rey Galang then relocated to the United States, and after relocating to New Jersey in 1992, started the first official classes of kalis Ilustrisimo, under the Bakbakan International banner, in the United States. He now runs a full-time training hall in Lodi, New Jersey.

During the 1990s, the late Edgar Sulite relocated to California and perpetuated the art of kalis Ilustrisimo through his own lameco eskrima system. Although not the focus of his art, the name and techniques of the Ilustrisimo system were nonetheless spread and promoted through the vast efforts of Edgar Sulite.

In 1996, Mark Wiley also began teaching kalis Ilustrisimo, and he has since taught the art in Boston, Philadelphia, Princeton, and Baltimore in addition to Japan and England. In 1998 Mark invited Christopher Ricketts, Tony Diego, and Alex Co to come to the United States to make a series of instructional videos on kalis Ilustrisimo, sagasa, ngo cho kun, and praying mantis kung fu for Unique Publications Video. Although Diego could not travel because of a high workload, Ricketts and Co did come, and aside from filming the videos, taught a number of classes and seminars in New Jersey, Pennsylvania, and California.

Antonio Diego with JKD/kali instructor Burton Richardson, after a private lesson

Aside from Galang, Sulite, and Wiley, a number of other individuals have traveled to the Philippines from the United States to study the art over the years, including Michael Belzer, Burton Richardson, and Vincen Poques.

The Talim Ilustrisimo Orihinal (Repeticion) group (standing, L to R)
Cleri Gan, Andrew Kong, Master David Chan of Hsin-I,
Grandmaster Antonio Diego, Thomas Dy Tang, Francis Capinpin,
Fredie Yu. (kneeling, L to R) Henry Ong, Ruel So

In addition to the Philippines, Australia, and the United States, arnis practitioners from a number of other countries have also come to the Philippines to study the art of kalis Ilustrisimo. Among them are Gerry Gallano of Canada, Shamin Menul Haque, Abjol Miah, and Serge Gillete of France.

The Bakbakan International Group, Philippines

Various teachers of the art (standing L to R) Roberto Morales, Grandmaster
Ilustrisimo, Norman Suaneco (kneeling), Mark V. Wiley, Pedro Reyes

Since the death of Antonio Ilustrisimo in 1997, there has been much rivalry and dispute among the senior students as to who is teaching the "correct" system of their late master. Politics aside, and in fairness to all, there are currently several groups teaching the art in the Philippines, including: Talim Ilustrisimo Orihinal "Repeticion" (headed by Antonio Diego), Bakbakan International (headed by Christopher Ricketts), Tagpas Kali Ilustrisimo (headed by Romeo Macapagal), Pamantukan (headed by Yuli Room), Kali Combatant (headed by Pedring Romo), Luneta Kali Ilustrisimo (headed Pedro Reyes and Samuel Ilustrisimo), and Olistrisimo Eskrima (headed by Roberto Morales).

CHAPTER TWO

Structure of the
Ilustrisimo System

CLASSIFICATION OF THE SYSTEM

As an art, kalis Ilustrisimo is difficult to classify. Since it embraces many of the sword techniques of pre-Hispanic times, the classical espada y daga style of the Spanish era, and the systematization and teaching structure of our modern times, it is at once an ancient, classical, and modern style of arnis. More importantly, kalis Ilustrisimo can be viewed as a microcosm of the Filipino arts in general, because it continually evolves to suit the times and needs of its practitioners.

Although grounded in sword techniques, kalis Ilustrisimo is a complete fighting art because it encompasses many types and classifications of weapon and empty-hand techniques. In edged weapons, the art trains the single sword (Figure 2.1), double swords (Figure 2.2), single knife (Figure 2.3), and concurrent use of a sword and dagger (Figure 2.4). In impact weapons, the art trains the single stick (Figure 2.5), double sticks (Figure 2.6), and staff (Figure 2.7). In flexible weapons, the art trains the rope, chain, and handkerchief (Figure 2.8). In empty-hand fighting, the art trains various parries, locks, and disarms (Figure 2.9).

Figure 2.1

Figure 2.2

Figure 2.3

Figure 2.4

Figure 2.5

Figure 2.6

Figure 2.7

Figure 2.8

Figure 2.9

In terms of weapon use, kalis Ilustrisimo employs them solo and in pairs, single- and double-handed. Moreover, every technique that is used for the sword can be applied to the stick, staff, and knife, with appropriate adjustments and with proper training. Thus, the art is compact in terms of its number of techniques, but comprehensive in terms of employing those techniques in a variety of ways and with a variety of weapons. In essence, and regardless of technique or weapon used, the art favors direct striking and disabling, and has no time for showmanship, excess movement, or lock and control techniques that don't end an altercation immediately.

At first glance, kalis Ilustrisimo appears to be similar to the other arnis systems. But, as they say, looks can be deceiving. In terms of fighting philosophy and strategy, the Ilustrisimo style is radically different from the others. In particular, it is sword-based and not stick-based, makes use of a wider variety of weapons than most styles of arnis, and makes use of dynamic body mechanics (as opposed to mere arm swinging) and intricate footwork and angling (as opposed to the standard two triangle steps). Moreover, the art does not condone *lawhag,* or wide movements, but stresses economy of movement, strategic positioning, and use of weapon and centerline awareness. In addition, the art stresses broken rhythm and unusual counters that tend to confuse even masters of other arnis systems. This is based on the idea of "praksion," or being a fraction of a second faster than your opponent, and being only a fraction of a distance away from the danger of a strike, thus wasting no movement and increasing speed and timing of counters.

PROGRESSIONS IN TRAINING

While there is traditionally no specific progression in learning this art, Antonio Ilustrisimo often stated that students should begin their training with the double sticks. This, he said, would concurrently train both their left and right arms and coordination from the onset, thus giving them some semblance of skill with their weaker limb, should the need arise.

However, over the years a general teaching guideline has evolved, if only intuitively, and it begins with the single stick—because it is the most common weapon used in arnis today. When new students begin training, they are first taught how to measure and hold their weapon, then how to stand. From there, footwork is introduced, followed by the system's twelve angles of attack and eleven basic striking "styles," which are then trained concurrently with the footwork.

Once a strong foundation is built, students are taught the basic counter techniques, such as *estrella, vertical, pluma,* and so on, and then the various striking styles used as follow-ups, such as *rompida, planchada, aldabis,* and so on. At this time, one person strikes at another, who in turn counters with a defensive technique and follow-up striking combination.

After some time, the students will begin free-flow drilling of their techniques, which resembles sparring inasmuch as it is not prearranged. This drilling finds one person striking another in various combinations and the defender doing his best to apply his defensive stick and hand parries and counters

(Figures 2.10 and 2.11). This free-flow drill then becomes the nucleus of the system, from which the skills of disarming are taught.

Figure 2.10

Figure 2.11

After the students have developed their foundation and have perfected their techniques with the single stick, they are often free to choose which weapon to learn next. Most of the time, however, the double sticks will be next, followed by single sword, sword and dagger, and staff. The skills in the handkerchief, double swords, two-handed sword, and empty hands are taught intermittently at the instructor's discretion.

Regardless of the weapon employed, when training with a stick, always treat it as if it were a bolo. In this way, every defense will be correct, and you will not have to change your stick movements into blade movements should the situation arise.

TRAINING METHODS

Where training methods are concerned, it is better to have only a few drills, but ones that concentrate on developing the skills necessary to be able to apply your art in real encounters, such as: coordination, speed, timing, distancing, power, conditioning, and proper mind set.

To develop coordination, double sticks are twirled in various combinations of vertical, diagonal, horizontal, and circular motions. In addition a single stick exercise, known as *amara,* is taught, whose movements resemble the intricate weave of a floor mat. Amara is an "alive hand" drill, which coordinates the movements and positioning of both the empty and weapon hands and leads to efficiency and strategic advantage in controlling openings and setting up disarms. Amara can also be used as a set of prefight movements.

To develop power, striking a car tire hung from the ceiling or mounted to the wall is quite effective and is akin to a boxer punching a heavy bag to develop impact power and endurance. The tire is also useful for developing the proper mechanics of striking with both stick and sword, and especially correct wrist positioning with a sword, because if it is incorrect, the practitioner will feel pain on impact.

A sense of timing, coordination, good reflexes, and distancing are concurrently developed through the free-flow drills, which find one partner striking at random, while the other responds in kind and counters (Figure 2.12).

Figure 2.12

After Ricketts suggested that the Ilustrisimo group could improve their fighting skills through sparring, whenever they engaged in such practices, the sessions would end after one or two blows as a result of swollen hands and broken fingers. Until that time, the art was generally practiced only with live blades or hard sticks. In answer to this, Yuli Romo developed the first padded rattan stick, and Edgar Sulite developed the first form-fitting hand pads. As a result, from that point on they were able to train more realistically without experiencing crippling injuries at every turn.

The method of controlled sparring we developed as a result of this new equipment became known as target practice. This finds two practitioners facing off wearing a padded hand guard and wielding a padded rattan stick. The objective at first is to strike the opponent's weapon hand without being struck by his stick. It sounds easy, but it is not. There is but a single target, and both partners know where the other intends to strike; therefore, it's quite difficult to land a clean blow and retract your striking hand before being struck in return. The drill then progresses in target selection to include the legs. With such controlled and limited targets to strike—and all of them vital—it is easy to see how becoming proficient in such an environment is of benefit when applying the art in a real encounter.

After the above methods have been well trained, students then don head-gear and go at it full contact, anything goes. At this phase, students attempt to overcome one another with skill, technique, timing, distancing, strikes, disarms, sweeps, and takedowns.

PART II

Fundamentals of Practice

Preliminaries

Now that you have an understanding of the history, development, structure, and training methods of kalis Ilustrisimo, we can proceed to its fighting techniques. But before delving into the nuts and bolts of the art, a foundation must be built. The preliminary areas that must be addressed prior to beginning the physical practice of the art are: how to find the proper length of the weapon you will employ, how to properly grip the weapon, and an understanding of the conceptual nature of the three primary combat ranges.

WEAPON LENGTH

Today, the length of the stick used in arnis around the world has become a standardized twenty-four to twenty-six inches. However, practitioners of kalis Ilustrisimo feel the use of such standard sizes can do the practitioner more harm than good, because the weapon should fit the individual.

In kalis Ilustrisimo, the proper length of the single-handed weapon you should employ is determined in one of two ways (both of which yield the same measurement). The first method is by holding the weapon in front of your body at shoulder height, with both hands gripping it in its center. The correct length is determined anatomically by the distance from elbow to elbow (Figure 3.1).

Figure 3.1

The second method used to determine the appropriate length is to hold the weapon at one end, with the thumb and pinkie of your extended arm, against your armpit. The correct length is determined anatomically by the distance from your armpit to the tips of the fingers of your outstretched arm (Figure 3.2).

For two-handed weapons, such as the long sword or staff, the length is determined by measuring the distance from the floor to your sternum and from the floor to the top of your head, respectively.

By adjusting the length of the weapon to an individual's body size, the kalis Ilustrisimo practitioner is able to effectively maneuver the weapon, while at the same time decreasing the chances of inadvertently striking himself in the process (Figure 3.3).

Figure 3.2

Figure 3.3

WEAPON GRIP

There are several ways to grip your weapon; which is appropriate is largely dependent on the circumstances and range in which you find yourself fighting.

The first method is the standard grip, known simply as *hawakan* (grip), wherein you hold the weapon at one end, with the majority of its length protruding past the thumb. In this position, the hand can either grip the weapon flush against its *punyo* (butt end) (Figure 3.4)—which is preferred for long-to-medium-range techniques—or allow one to three inches of the punyo to protrude past the pinkie finger (Figure 3.5)—which allows for striking, locking, and disarming with the butt end at close quarters.

The second gripping method (as long as the weapon is blunt!) is to hold it in its middle. This is known as *centro baston,* because the stick is held in its center, or middle (Figure 3.6). And while this grip allows both ends of the weapon to be used equally in attack and defense, because of poor leverage it is not as effective as the standard grip. It is nonetheless important to learn how to employ your techniques from this position, because who can predict just how one will pick up or acquire a weapon at the onset of an altercation?

Figure 3.4

Figure 3.5

Figure 3.6

The third gripping method finds the weapon in the exact opposite position to the standard grip. In this grip, the weapon is inverted, and the majority of its length protrudes past the pinkie finger (Figure 3.7). This grip is known as *susi* (key), because the position resembles the way in which one might hold one's keys when opening a lock. This grip is also less preferable than the standard grip because of the somewhat awkward body mechanics needed to effectively employ the art's techniques from this position. However, the grip allows you to walk with the stick concealed along the back of your forearm, thus giving you the element of surprise if you're mugged, because the attacker will not suspect you are armed.

Figure 3.7

Once the techniques of kalis Ilustrisimo are learned from the standard-grip weapon position, it is a necessity that they all be relearned and perfected using the other two grip positions. This will ensure one's ability to defend oneself from any weapon position, at least long enough to switch grips to the preferred standard grip.

COMBAT RANGES

There are three primary fighting distances, or combat ranges, as defined in kalis Ilustrisimo: long, medium, and close. It is important to understand, though, that these ranges are conceptually based and determined by the length of your arms and weapon in relation to those of your opponents. So, depending on the height of your opponent and the length of weapon he employs, what may be long range for you may be medium range for him. However, what range your opponent is fighting from is less important than the range you find yourself fighting in and the techniques you employ therein.

It is imperative that you develop the ability to immediately intuit the range in which you are fighting and employ the appropriate technique. This can be done by measuring the combat ranges as described below against opponents of various sizes and weapon lengths. In this way you will be better prepared to effectively apply your techniques in the correct range at the appropriate moment.

Each style of arnis has its own terms and definitions of what constitutes various combat ranges. In kalis Ilustrisimo, long range is known as *de campo,* because it is indicative of the style of "play" employed in an open field. The range is determined by the furthest distance at which you can strike your opponent's furthest extended limb (most often the hand holding the weapon). The distance is measured by facing a partner and both of you extending your weapon arm and weapon far enough away that only the top four to six inches of your weapon (that is, the striking or cutting portion) can touch the other's hand (Figure 3.8).

Figure 3.8

In kalis Ilustrisimo, medium range is known as *de medio,* because it is the middle distance between the long and close ranges. Medium range is determined by the distance at which you can strike your opponent's body with your weapon and also check, disarm, or parry his weapon hand. However, at this range, you are too far away to strike an opponent's head or body with your empty hand (at least without moving). The distance is measured by facing your partner and both of you extending your arms with your weapons held upright. Stand close enough together that the fingers of your respective weapon hands are facing each other's inner wrist (Figure 3.9).

In kalis Ilustrisimo, close range is known as *de salon,* because such a distance is indicative of the space available in which to maneuver in a salon or living quarters. Close range (also known as close quarters) is determined by the distance at which you can strike your opponent's head and body with both your weapon and your empty hand. The distance is measured by facing your partner and extending your arms out in front of you with your weapon held upright. Stand close enough together that your clenched fist can touch your opponent's shoulder (Figure 3.10).

Figure 3.9

Figure 3.10

While these are the three primary combat ranges as conceptualized in kalis Ilustrisimo, bear in mind that range does not necessitate specific target selection, because desired targets can and do vary in combat as openings are offered or created. As an example, Antonio Ilustrisimo was fond of hitting his opponent's hands, even when in close range.

Stances and Footwork

Any weapons-based fighting art must employ the skills of footwork and eva-
sion to a high degree. A person cannot simply stand still and allow himself to
be struck by his opponent's weapons—especially if those weapons are sharp.
As a weapon-based art, the techniques and timing of its exponents must be
precise. The foundation of such precision is rooted in the development of
proper stances and footwork, of which there are ten in kalis Ilustrisimo. It is
proper body positioning and footwork that allow the practitioner of this art
to at once be in a position to strike his opponent, while at the same time evad-
ing or simply being out of range of the opponent's weapon.

The fighting stances and footwork of kalis Ilustrisimo are based on two
primary premises: (1) that exponents of this style prefer to wait for their opponent to attack before moving and countering, believing that this will offer
them an opening in which to counter; and (2) that since medium range is the
preferred fighting distance, the art's footwork should accommodate methods
of moving out of the range when necessary and then immediately moving
back into it. As a result, the footwork in this style is defensively based, and

often involves leaning back, stepping back or on an angle, or shifting the body backward or at an angle prior to making a forward body movement.

The following is an introduction to the fundamentals of posture and movement that underlie and make effective the techniques of this art.

TINDIG ABIERTA

There is really only one stance in kalis Ilustrisimo, and it is called *tindig abierta,* or open-guard stance. It is the primary ready position assumed when facing an opponent. The stance is akin to a boxing stance, finding the practitioner standing with one leg a natural step in front of the other, the heel of the back foot raised, hands held up at head level, and elbows held close to the ribs. In this position, the stick is held vertically and in line with the shoulder of the stick–wielding arm, thus the figurative door is "open" (Figure 4.1).

Figure 4.1

This fighting stance is so basic and simple that practitioners of other arts fail to see its merit. However, if we analyze the stance we find that the standing position is natural to the human body, the lifted rear heel aids in mobility without wasting time raising or lowering your knees or feet prior to moving, the hands are held in such a way as to protect the head and body at all times, and the stick is held from the onset in the starting position of the most basic and common forehand vertical or diagonal strike. Thus, the stance has much intrinsic value.

If we now consider the more classical stances of other styles of arnis, we see that the empty hand is often held in the center of the body in front of the chest. This is not a desirable position for two reasons: that hand becomes the primary target of the opponent, and one develops the bad habit of raising that hand to block an oncoming strike rather than parrying the opponent's weapon from the outside. In addition, the deeply bent knee or crossed leg positions of many styles reduce mobility, speed of movement, and the ability to drop the body weight into a strike to increase its power, since the body is already low.

TINDIG SERRADA

The secondary fighting stance in kalis Ilustrisimo is called *tindig serrada,* or closed-guard stance. This stance is assumed in much the same manner as the previous stance, the difference being the position of the weapon. In this stance, the stick-wielding arm is held across the body, with the stick pointing behind the exponent, thus the figurative door is "closed" (Figure 4.2).

This fighting stance is less desirable than the open-guard stance when facing an opponent, because it not only limits the offensive and defensive options but also offers your opponent your forearm and elbow as a primary target. However, the position is quite effective in an immediate attacking advance, because the backhand strike is quite powerful and often difficult to block as a first movement.

Figure 4.2

DE ELASTIKO

This technique belongs to the classical style of arnis. Like a piece of elastic (or a rubber band) that expands and contracts when stretched, the *de elastiko* movement allows a practitioner to weave his body in and out of combat ranges without actually taking a step. It is actually neither a stance nor a footwork, but rather a method of moving (weaving) back and forth between close, medium, and long ranges. Specifically, de elastiko is a method of moving out of range of an oncoming strike while simultaneously striking the opponent's attacking limb, and then moving back into range to counterattack.

To perform de elastiko, assume the abierta stance, this time with your weapon held low (Figure 4.3). As a strike nears, shift your weight back onto your rear leg while simultaneously straightening your front leg, so that the foot rests on its heel, and swinging your weapon upward (Figure 4.4). Once you have simultaneously moved out of striking distance and directly struck your opponent's attacking arm, weave your body forward, simultaneously shifting your weight onto your front leg, straightening your rear leg, and striking downward (Figure 4.5).

Figure 4.3

Figure 4.4

Figure 4.5

The strength of this movement is that it accommodates the simultaneous movement off a line of attack with directly striking the opponent's attacking limb, thus making it fast and economical. Its limitation, however, is that it is difficult to perform for older practitioners or those with "bad knees." In addition, if it is used too much, it affords a perceptive opponent the opportunity to time your movements and thus counter them. But, as the saying goes, there's a time and place for everything.

RITERADA

The fundamental defensive footwork employed in kalis Ilustrisimo is called *riterada,* meaning "retreat." It is a natural shuffle step used to move the practitioner from medium to long range and then back to medium range in reaction to an opponent's strike.

To perform riterada, assume the abierta fighting stance (Figure 4.6). As a strike nears, take a step back with your rear leg (Figure 4.7) and then an equal step back with your front leg (Figure 4.8), thus moving out of the strike's range. Next, quickly step forward with your front leg (Figure 4.9) followed by an equal step forward with your rear leg (Figure 4.10), thus regaining distance and finishing in the same location in which you began.

Figure 4.6

Figure 4.7

Figure 4.8

Figure 4.9

Figure 4.10

It is important when shuffling forward or back that both feet move an equal distance so that at the end of the movement you retain your balance and proper fighting stance. It is also important to develop the skill of moving only enough to avoid being struck, as overstepping can result in lost time and inefficiency. This movement is the foundation on which the *equis* and *lutang* movements are based.

EQUIS

Equis refers to the letter X, and adds an X-shaped or crossed-legged transitional movement to the riterada step. This added transitional movement aids the practitioner in moving into long range from close or medium range should an opponent's weapon be long or his strike particularly extended.

To perform equis, assume the abierta fighting stance (Figure 4.11). As a strike nears, turn your rear foot out and twist your hips counterclockwise

(Figure 4.12) while taking a full step back with your front leg (Figure 4.13). Once you have effectively moved out of the strike's range, take a full step forward with your front leg (Figure 4.14), thus regaining distance and finishing in the same location in which you began.

Figure 4.11

Figure 4.12

Figure 4.13

Figure 4.14

This footwork is especially useful when a last-minute movement is necessary to avoid a strike when the riterada step falls short of safety. Moreover, the dynamic twisting of the hips allows for a more powerful counterstrike as a result of the additional body mechanics involved.

LUTANG

Lutang means "floating" and is unique to the Ilustrisimo family art. It was the preferred footwork of Antonio Ilustrisimo because it allows one to remain in one place while moving one's body out of the way of an attack through the "floating" action of the lead leg.

To perform lutang, assume the abierta fighting stance (Figure 4.15). As a strike nears, either slide (Figure 4.16) or swing (Figure 4.17) your lead leg directly behind you and then forward again in a single motion (Figure 4.18), thus giving it the appearance of floating. Another method is to slide your leg back on a 45-degree angle (Figures 4.19 and 4.20).

While you can either lightly slide the front leg on the ground or "float it" without touching the ground, it is imperative that you place as little body weight on the "floating" leg as possible. Too much weight will slow its movement. Moreover, the direction in which you choose to move your leg will depend on the direction of your opponent's strike and where and how you intend to counterattack. In essence, your body should be aligned with your arm when striking.

Figure 4.15

Figure 4.16

Figure 4.17

Figure 4.18

Figure 4.19

Figure 4.20

Lutang is one of the most economical footwork/body maneuvers in kalis Ilustrisimo, because it not only moves your body out of range quickly but does so while allowing you to maintain your relative distance to your opponent. It is also effectively used in disarming because it allows you to offset your opponent's balance and move in to disarm him while remaining balanced yourself.

TATLONG BAO

Tatlong bao refers to three halved coconut shells, which, when placed on the ground, are used as "stepping stones." More figurative than literal, it refers to stepping between three locations or points of an inverted triangle or V shape. This footwork is used to maneuver to the outside of a strike, thus putting you in a safer place to counterattack without having to move substantially from your given position. There are two methods of stepping along the inverted triangle: moving up and then back, and moving back and then up.

To perform the first method, assume the abierta fighting stance (Figure 4.21). As a strike nears, step with your left leg to the upper-left point of the inverted triangle (Figure 4.22), and then step your right leg back to the apex of the triangle, where the left leg previously rested (Figure 4.23). Then repeat the motions on the opposite side, by stepping with your right leg to the upper-right point of the inverted triangle (Figure 4.24), and then stepping back with your left leg to the apex of the triangle, where the right leg previously rested (Figure 4.25). At the completion of each step, you should face your opponent on a 45-degree angle.

Figure 4.21

Figure 4.22

Figure 4.23

Figure 4.24

Figure 4.25

To perform the second method, assume the abierta fighting stance (Figure 4.26). As a strike nears, step back with your right leg to the apex of the inverted triangle (Figure 4.27), and then step forward with your left leg to the top-left corner of the triangle (Figure 4.28). Then repeat the motions on the opposite side by stepping back with your left leg to the apex of the triangle (Figure 4.29), and then stepping forward with your right leg to the top-right corner of the triangle (Figure 4.30). You are now back where you started.

This footwork is especially useful when you find yourself in a position where you can neither step back nor to the side, such as when you are cornered. It is also an economical method of maneuvering to the blind side of an opponent without giving up distance. The downside is that it is too slow to use repeatedly from side to side in an actual fight. However, when linked with equis or lutang, it is quite dynamic and effective.

Figure 4.26

Figure 4.27

Figure 4.28

Figure 4.29

Figure 4.30

COMBATE/TRANKADA HENERAL

Combate heneral and *trankada heneral* are types of footwork that attempt to maneuver the practitioner around an opponent, thus flanking him on his "blind" side. They are nearly identical to the tatlong bao footwork, the difference being in the width of the steps. Where tatlong bao maneuvers the practitioner along a 45-degree angle in front of the opponent, combate and trankada heneral place the practitioner on a 90-degree angle to the side or back of the opponent.

As a rule, combate heneral moves the practitioner in the same direction that the oncoming strike is traveling. Thus, if a strike was traveling from your right to your left, you would leap 90 degrees to the left with your left leg, followed by your right leg. Conversely, trankada heneral moves the practitioner in the opposite direction of the oncoming strike. Thus, if a strike was traveling from your right to your left, you would leap 90 degrees to the right with your right leg, followed by your left leg.

DOBLETE

Doblete is a method of employing short, stomping steps in rapid succession in an effort to make quick and minor adjustments in your body position relative to your opponent, while distracting or confusing him in the process. In addition, the stomping action also acts as an anchor to ensure that at the moment one of your strikes or blocks makes impact your body is firmly rooted to the ground.

Methods of Striking

Like many styles of eskrima and arnis, kalis Ilustrisimo employs a set of twelve strikes, known generally as the "angles of attack." These strikes are predetermined and travel along specified angles or paths of movement, along which any type of attack is thought likely to fall. While there is a set sequence to the twelve strikes, it is not looked on as an attacking pattern but as a training tool through which one learns where to strike an opponent and, when facing a partner who is striking, how to block and counter the same strikes. This sequence of strikes does nothing more than act to simplify instruction: for example, one can say, "feed me angle five," and one's partner will know what to do, rather than saying, "can you attack me with a forward thrust to my midsection."

ANATOMY OF A STRIKE

Perhaps more important than the sequence of the twelve strikes is understanding the components of each strike. These are the elements that make them effective; they include: body mechanics, gripping action, intention, precision, and timing. Without proper development of these areas a strike, regardless of its angle, will lack power and integrity.

Regarding proper body mechanics, keep in mind that a strike executed with the arm alone is only as strong as that arm, whereas a strike executed with the weight and structure of the entire body behind it is as strong as that combined body unit. As a general rule, then, when striking down you must drop your weight, when striking up you must raise your hips, and when striking horizontally or thrusting you must twist your hips accordingly. Moreover, your body must be properly aligned in the direction of a given strike. That is, your shoulders, hips, and feet must move in the direction of the strike in tandem with the striking arm motion.

Aside from the three aforementioned ways of holding a weapon, the way you grip it when striking is also important. First, always assume that you are holding and maneuvering a bladed weapon. In this way, you will develop the proper arm and wrist action when striking, regardless of whether you hold a sword or stick. Second, never hold your weapon too tightly, because this will at once fatigue you and slow your movements. It is best to hold the weapon tightly with the thumb and first two fingers and loosely with the last two fingers while preparing to strike. To generate power on impact, grip tightly with the last two fingers while accordingly sinking or raising your body weight.

Regarding intention, you should have no facial expression when striking. When you grit your teeth, you are not only tensing your body, and thus slowing your movements, but showing your opponent when you intend to strike, thus forgoing the element of surprise. You should be calm and focused at all times and never telegraph your intentions. Be focused on your opponent, intent on striking him when and where you like, and always be precise in movement because any wasted motion can lead to inadvertent defeat.

The Angles of Attack

In the classic eskrima system of the Ilustrisimo family, there are two sets of twelve strikes: one from the abierta fighting stance and one from serrada fighting stance. However, given Antonio Ilustrisimo's predominant use of the abierta stance, here we illustrate only the set of strikes from the open guard. Moreover, in keeping with simplicity and the continuity of the instructional material illustrated in this volume, tindig abierta is the position from which all of the techniques are later presented, so only one striking set is necessary for our purposes here.

As a quick reference, the strikes are as follows:

1. Diagonal Forehand Collarbone Strike
2. Diagonal Backhand Collarbone Strike
3. Horizontal Forehand Midsection Strike
4. Horizontal Backhand Midsection Strike
5. Direct Midsection Thrust
6. Backhand Thrust to Chest
7. Forehand Thrust to Chest
8. Backhand Thrust to Midsection
9. Vertical Forehand Upward Strike
10. Backhand Thrust to Eye
11. Forehand Thrust to Eye
12. Vertical Downward Backhand Strike (Assisted)

When executing the twelve strikes, you will maneuver between each by utilizing the tatlong bao footwork. This will ensure that your lead leg matches the side from which each strike initiates, thus teaching you the proper distance and mechanics of each strike. In addition, it is important to keep in mind that there should be no pause between each striking motion, because the end of one motion is the beginning of the next.

Begin the sequence by assuming the abierta stance and facing a passive partner (Figure 5.1). For strike one, strike diagonally down from right to left on the opponent's left collarbone (Figure 5.2).

Figure 5.1

Figure 5.2

Strike two begins at the end of the previous strike's motion, as you change steps (Figure 5.3). While in transition, strike diagonally down from left to right to the opponent's right ribs area (Figure 5.4).

Figure 5.3

Figure 5.4

Strike three begins at the end of the previous strike's motion, as you change steps (Figure 5.5). While in transition, strike diagonally down from right to left to the opponent's left ribs area (Figure 5.6).

Figure 5.5

Figure 5.6

Strike four begins at the end of the previous strike's motion, as you change steps (Figure 5.7). While in transition, strike diagonally down from left to right to the opponent's right collarbone (Figure 5.8).

Figure 5.7

Figure 5.8

Strike five begins at the end of the previous strike's motion, as you change steps (Figure 5.9). While in transition, thrust the tip of your weapon forward to your opponent's navel area (Figure 5.10).

Figure 5.9

Figure 5.10

Strike six begins at the end of the previous strike's motion, as you change steps (Figure 5.11). While in transition, thrust the tip of your weapon to your the opponent's right chest area (Figure 5.12).

Figure 5.11

Figure 5.12

Strike seven begins at the end of the previous strike's motion, as you change steps (Figure 5.13). While in transition, thrust the tip of your weapon to your the opponent's left chest area (Figure 5.14).

Figure 5.13

Figure 5.14

Strike eight begins at the end of the previous strike's motion, as you change steps (Figure 5.15). While in transition, thrust the tip of your weapon to your the opponent's right ribs area (Figure 5.16).

Figure 5.15

Figure 5.16

Strike nine begins at the end of the previous strike's motion, as you change steps (Figure 5.17). While in transition, strike vertically from the ground up the opponent's midsection (Figure 5.18).

Figure 5.17

Figure 5.18

Strike ten begins at the end of the previous strike's motion, as you change steps (Figure 5.19). While in transition, thrust the tip of your weapon to the opponent's right eye (Figure 5.20).

Figure 5.19

Figure 5.20

Strike eleven begins at the end of the previous strike's motion, as you change steps (Figure 5.21). While in transition, thrust the tip of your weapon to the opponent's left eye (Figure 5.22).

Figure 5.21

Figure 5.22

Strike twelve begins at the end of the previous strike's motion, as you change steps (Figure 5.23). While in transition, use your left hand to assist a downward, overhead strike to the crown of your opponent's head (Figure 5.24).

Figure 5.23

Figure 5.24

STRIKING "STYLES"

Unlike other systems of arnis, wherein their practitioners only learn defenses against the number and sequence of their respective angles of attack, kalis Ilustrisimo trains its practitioners to defend against and attack with a variety of striking "styles" not found in the basic series of twelve strikes. When training for fighting, various combinations of single and paired weapons are manipulated horizontally, vertically, diagonally, and along the X shape, V shape, and O shape. This allows the practitioner to become familiar with various striking motions and how to move from one into another at the conclusion of a strike's natural motion.

The following eleven striking styles each have their own name and unique properties. They at once familiarize the practitioner with additional striking motions not found in the preset twelve strikes and, when combined with the defensive movements illustrated in chapter 6, become counterattacking techniques. Moreover, kalis Ilustrisimo is a dynamic and responsive art—there are no fighting combinations to memorize. The defensive movements (for example, estrella, pluma, and so on) are combined with the striking styles (for example, *planchada, bagsak,* and so on) to form innumerable fighting combinations. And it is the dynamic of the altercation that will dictate which combinations of defensive movements, footwork, and striking styles will be employed. The striking styles are:

Vertical	Forehand and backhand vertical strikes along the opponent's center line
Equis	Forehand and backhand diagonal strikes
Planchada	Back and forth horizontal strikes from the opponent's collarbone to waist
Aldabis	Forehand and backhand upward diagonal strikes from the opponent's waist to collarbone

Rompida	Up and down vertical slashes
De cadena	Forehand and backhand collarbone strikes repeated twice in succession on each side
Bagsak	Forehand and backhand downward strikes with body weight
Sunod sampal	Horizontal side-to-side swinging stick strikes
Abaniko	Diagonal fanning strikes from temple to midsection or midsection to temple
Tusuk	Forehand, backhand, and direct thrusts
Sonkite	A thrust and slash combination

PART III

Defensive Movements and Applications

CHAPTER SIX

Fundamental
Fighting Techniques

In executing the techniques of kalis Ilustrisimo, always keep your weapon
held close to your body, which not only keeps you well protected but allows
for fast and efficient movement. It is also important to move off the line of
attack and reposition yourself, while at the same time remaining in an appropriate range from which to counterattack.

Regardless of the weapon you practice with, always assume that you and
your opponent are both armed with bladed weapons. In this way, you do not
have to consider whether or not it is suitable to use the blunt weapon version
of a given technique, because you will automatically perform the bladed version. Although it takes more practice to perform the techniques in the bladed
fashion, it is simply the safest way, not to mention the original intent of the
techniques.

For illustration purposes, and considering the space limitations of a book, only a sampling of the fighting techniques of kalis Ilustrisimo are illustrated below. Moreover, they are only applied here against diagonal and horizontal forehand and backhand strikes, because these are the most common. Keep in mind, however, that the techniques are certainly applicable against a variety of different strikes. Thus, to get the most benefit from your training, experiment with applying these techniques against each of the twelve angles of attack and also incorporate the eleven striking styles into your follow-up counters.

The following is a description and depiction of the thirteen fundamental defensive fighting techniques of kalis Ilustrisimo.

ESTRELLA

Estrella refers to the star shape made when the weapons of the attacker and defender clash. It is a counter technique best used against horizontal blows, because employing it against diagonal blows may seriously injure your hand. When checking with your left hand, it should be held flat, palm facing down, and placed on the web of the attacker's hand. Aside from the obvious check and blocking support, the hand is used for pulling in the opponent, disarming, and joint locking. The tip of your weapon should be pointing straight up, and the stick and hand should engage the opponent in the same moment.

Stick Application: Square off with your opponent in the abierta fighting stance (Figure 6.1). As the opponent initiates a horizontal stick strike, step to the right using the tatlong bao footwork while simultaneously parrying his stick with your vertically held stick and checking the top of his weapon hand with your left hand (Figure 6.2). While maintaining a hold on his weapon hand and pushing it away slightly, continue your stick's natural motion and execute a diagonal counter strike to the opponent's midsection (Figure 6.3).

Figure 6.1

Figure 6.2

Figure 6.3

Sword Application: Square off with your opponent in the abierta fighting stance (Figure 6.4). As the opponent initiates a horizontal sword slash, step to the right using the tatlong bao footwork while simultaneously parrying his sword with either the left or right flat edge of your sword (Figures 6.5 and 6.6) and checking the top of his weapon hand with your left hand (Figure 6.7). While maintaining a hold on his weapon hand and pushing it away slightly, continue your sword's natural motion and diagonally slash the opponent's midsection (Figures 6.8 and 6.9), followed by a thrust to his heart (Figure 6.10).

Figure 6.4

Figure 6.5

Figure 6.6

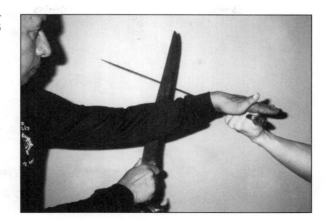

Figure 6.7

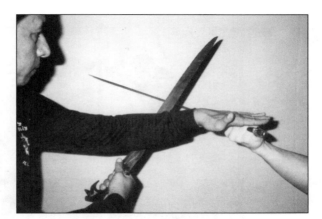

Figure 6.8

Figure 6.9

Figure 6.10

Sword and Dagger Application: Square off with your opponent in the abierta fighting stance (Figure 6.11). As the opponent initiates a horizontal sword slash, step to the right using the tatlong bao footwork while simultaneously parrying his sword with the flat edge of your sword (Figure 6.12) and thrusting your dagger into his sternum (Figure 6.13). This is immediately followed by a simultaneous diagonal sword slash to the opponent's midsection while your dagger maintains a check on the opponent's sword (Figure 6.14).

Figure 6.11

Figure 6.12

Figure 6.13

Figure 6.14

VERTICAL

Vertical is a technique whose structure is opposite that of estrella. While the weapon is held vertically, in this case the tip of the weapon points toward the ground. It is a counter technique best used against vertical and diagonal downward blows. In using this technique, you must anticipate your opponent's blow so as to move in slightly ahead of him and move your hips forward to aid in the stability of the technique's deflective action.

Stick Application: Square off with your opponent in the abierta fighting stance (Figure 6.15). As the opponent initiates a forehand downward strike with his stick, step toward the strike while simultaneously raising your stick so that the base of your opponent's stick meets the top portion of yours while checking his weapon hand with your left hand (Figure 6.16). The force of your opponent's strike will cause your stick to swing around (Figure 6.17), allowing you to counter with a vertical strike down his midsection (Figure 6.18).

Figure 6.15

Figure 6.16

Figure 6.17

Figure 6.18

Sword Application: Square off with your opponent in the abierta fighting stance (Figure 6.19). As the opponent initiates a forehand downward sword slash, step toward the strike while simultaneously raising your sword so that the base of your opponent's blade meets the flat edge of yours, and check his weapon hand with your left hand (Figures 6.20 and 6.21). The force of your opponent's strike will cause your sword to swing around (Figure 6.22), allowing you to counter with a vertical slash down his midsection (Figure 6.23).

Figure 6.19

Figure 6.20

Figure 6.21

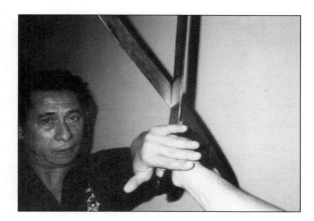

Figure 6.22

Figure 6.23

Sword and Dagger Application: Square off with your opponent in the abierta fighting stance (Figure 6.24). As the opponent initiates a forehand downward sword slash, shift your stance so that you stand perpendicular to him while simultaneously intercepting the blade of his sword with the flat edge of yours and thrusting your dagger into his midsection (Figure 6.25). Follow up by using your dagger to check his striking arm while allowing the force of your opponent's blow to redirect your sword (Figure 6.26). Reposition your body so that you are again facing your opponent while pushing his sword away from you with your dagger and slashing vertically down his center (Figure 6.27).

Figure 6.24

Figure 6.25

Figure 6.26

Figure 6.27

PLUMA

Pluma means "pen" and describes the position of the weapon as it is used, similar to that of holding a pen and writing. The technique is used to strike, parry, and redirect diagonal and horizontal attacks in a single motion. It must be noted, however, that this technique is intended for close-to-medium-range defensive maneuvering and is not structured to take the force of a long-range blow.

Stick Application: Square off with your opponent in the abierta fighting stance (Figure 6.28). As the opponent initiates a forehand stick strike, use the tatlong bao footwork to reposition your body while simultaneously parrying the back of his weapon hand with your left hand and striking the inside wrist of his striking arm with your stick (Figure 6.29). While continuing to parry his hand with yours, allow the momentum of his blow to redirect your stick (Figure 6.30), allowing you to effectively follow up with a horizontal or diagonal backhand strike to his face (Figure 6.31).

Figure 6.28

Figure 6.29

Figure 6.30

Figure 6.31

Sword Application: Square off with your opponent in the abierta fighting stance (Figure 6.32). As the opponent initiates a forehand sword slash, use the tatlong bao footwork to reposition your body while simultaneously parrying the back of his weapon hand with your left hand and cutting the wrist of his striking arm with your sword (Figure 6.33). (Which, in itself, should cripple the attacker). While continuing to parry his hand with yours, allow the momentum of his blow to redirect your sword (Figure 6.34), allowing you to effectively follow up with a horizontal or diagonal backhand slash to his face (Figure 6.35).

Figure 6.32

Figure 6.33

Figure 6.34

Figure 6.35

Sword and Dagger Application: Square off with your opponent in the abierta fighting stance (Figure 6.36). As the opponent initiates a forehand sword slash, use the tatlong bao footwork to reposition your body while simultaneously parrying/cutting the back of his weapon hand with the dagger in your left hand and cutting the wrist of his striking arm with your sword (Figure 6.37). The momentum of his blow allows your sword to maneuver around his weapon and slash his neck or head while you thrust your dagger into his waist (Figure 6.38).

Figure 6.36

Figure 6.37

Figure 6.38

FLORETE

Florete refers to a fencer's foil, and this technique resembles the movements of a foil fencer. Using the left hand as a brace on the back of the weapon, in one motion the attacker's oncoming weapon is parried and redirected, at which point the defender's weapon continues on to counterthrust. This technique is best used against horizontal and diagonal blows, and requires excellent timing, precise body mechanics, and acute sensitivity of touch.

Stick Application: Square off with your opponent in the abierta fighting stance (Figure 6.39). As your opponent initiates a forehand stick strike, intercept it with your stick in a position similar to estrella while placing the knife edge of your left hand on the back of your stick as a brace (Figure 6.40). This looks like a force-on-force block, but it is not. Immediately on impact, step back with your right leg to move your body off the line of attack while redirecting your opponent's stick down and to the right with your hand-supported stick (Figure 6.41). Once his stick has been moved past you, close the distance again by stepping forward with your right leg while thrusting your stick into his sternum (Figure 6.42).

Figure 6.39

Figure 6.40

Figure 6.41

Figure 6.42

Sword Application: Square off with your opponent in the abierta fighting stance (Figure 6.43). As the opponent initiates a forehand sword slash, intercept it with the flat edge of your sword in a position similar to estrella while placing the knife edge of your left hand on the opposite flat edge of your sword as a brace (Figure 6.44). Immediately on impact, step back with your right leg to move your body off the line of attack while redirecting your opponent's sword down and to the right with your hand-supported sword (Figure 6.45). As his sword continues past you, step forward again with your right foot to close the distance while allowing your sword motion to move forward to slash the forearm of the opponent's weapon arm (Figure 6.46).

Figure 6.43

Figure 6.44

Figure 6.45

Figure 6.46

Sword and Dagger Application: Square off with your opponent in the abierta fighting stance (Figure 6.47). As the opponent initiates a forehand sword slash, intercept it with the flat edge of your sword, while pointing your dagger directly toward your opponent (Figure 6.48). Immediately on impact, employ the tatlong bao footwork to move your body off the line of attack while simultaneously redirecting your opponent's sword down and to the right and thrusting your dagger into his heart (Figure 6.49).

Figure 6.47

Figure 6.48

Figure 6.49

DOBLE CARERA

Doble carera refers to a double race, because one of your hands is figuratively chasing the other during the movements of the technique. This technique requires fast footwork and precise timing, because you are moving in the same direction that the opponent's strike is traveling and attempting to strike his head and attacking arm in the same motion. This technique works best against high, horizontal blows.

Stick Application: Square off with your opponent in the abierta fighting stance (Figure 6.50). As the opponent initiates a horizontal stick strike to your head, employ the combate heneral footwork to maneuver to his left side while striking his head (Figure 6.51) and then arm (Figure 6.52) in the same motion. Immediately after striking his arm, check his wrist with your left hand to keep his weapon from hitting you while thrusting your stick into his eyes (Figure 6.53).

Figure 6.50

Figure 6.51

Figure 6.52

Figure 6.53

Sword Application: Square off with your opponent in the abierta fighting stance (Figure 6.54). As the opponent initiates a horizontal sword slash to your head, employ the combate heneral footwork to maneuver to his left side while slashing his head (Figure 6.55) and then arm (Figure 6.56) in the same motion. Immediately after slashing his arm, check his wrist with your left hand to keep his weapon from hitting you while thrusting your sword into his face (Figure 6.57).

Figure 6.54

Figure 6.55

Figure 6.56

Figure 6.57

Sword and Dagger Application: Square off with your opponent in the abierta fighting stance (Figure 6.58). As the opponent initiates a horizontal sword slash to your head, employ the combate heneral footwork to maneuver to his left side while slashing his head (Figure 6.59) and then arm (Figure 6.60) in the same motion. Immediately after slashing his arm, check/cut his wrist with the dagger in your left hand while thrusting your sword into his face (Figure 6.61).

Figure 6.58

Figure 6.59

Figure 6.60

Figure 6.61

Media Fraile

Media fraile means "middle friar" and refers to the position of your and the opponent's weapon on impact, which resembles a friar's cross. Because this is the "middle" technique, you strike the opponent's hand with the middle of your weapon, which also happens to be positioned along the middle of the opponent's body. This is a shortened version of the ("full") fraile technique, which finds your weapon striking the opponent's head prior to his weapon hand. This is a medium-range technique that works best against downward forehand and backhand strikes.

Stick Application: Square off with your opponent in the abierta fighting stance (Figure 6.62). As the opponent initiates a vertical downward stick strike, simultaneously step your left foot to the top-left point of an inverted triangle while parrying his weapon hand with your left hand and striking his weapon hand with your stick (Figure 6.63). As your weapon completes its strike, your left hand continues to parry the weapon hand away from your body (Figure 6.64). While maintaining a check on your opponent's weapon hand, thrust your stick into his face (Figure 6.65).

Figure 6.62

Figure 6.63

Figure 6.64

Figure 6.65

Sword Application: Square off with your opponent in the abierta fighting stance (Figure 6.66). As the opponent initiates a vertical downward sword slash, simultaneously step your left foot to the top-left point of an inverted triangle while parrying his weapon hand with your left hand and checking the blade of his sword with the back edge of your sword or striking his hand with the back of your sword (Figure 6.67). (Unless you are using a double-edged sword, your sword cannot be used to slash his hand with this technique). Pull your sword past the opponent's sword while simultaneously parrying his weapon hand away from your body (Figure 6.68). While maintaining a check on your opponent's weapon hand, thrust your sword into his face or throat (Figure 6.69).

Figure 6.66

Figure 6.67

Figure 6.68

Figure 6.69

Sword and Dagger Application: Square off with your opponent in the abierta fighting stance (Figure 6.70). As the opponent initiates a vertical downward sword slash, simultaneously step your left foot to the top-left point of an inverted triangle while parrying/cutting his weapon hand with the dagger in your left hand and checking the blade of his sword with the back edge of your sword or striking his hand with the back of your sword (Figure 6.71). Pull your sword past the opponent's sword while simultaneously parrying his weapon hand away from your body (Figure 6.72). While maintaining a check on your opponent's weapon hand, thrust your sword into his face or throat (Figure 6.73).

Figure 6.70

Figure 6.71

Figure 6.72

Figure 6.73

BOCA DE LOBO

Boca de lobo is a technique wherein the empty hand and weapon move in such a way as to resemble the open mouth of a wolf. In applying the technique, you move in the direction of the oncoming strike while separating your weapon and empty hand on impact. There are two variations to this technique, one against a single opponent and the other against multiple opponents. In the latter case, the motion of the weapon is wider and the footwork more dynamic. This technique is best used against overhead strikes.

Stick Application: Square off with your opponent in the abierta fighting stance (Figure 6.74). As the opponent initiates an overhead stick strike, simultaneously step to your right while raising your stick and hand to intercept the opponent's stick and hand (Figure 6.75). Immediately on impact, extend your left hand to move your opponent's weapon away from you while circling your stick over and behind your head (Figure 6.76). While maintaining a check on the opponent's weapon hand, complete your stick's motion until it strikes the opponent's head (Figure 6.77).

Figure 6.74

Figure 6.75

Figure 6.76

Figure 6.77

Sword Application: Square off with your opponent in the abierta fighting stance (Figure 6.78). As the opponent initiates an overhead sword slash, simultaneously step to your right while intercepting the opponent's sword with the flat edge of your sword and his weapon hand with your left hand (Figure 6.79). Immediately on impact, extend your left hand to move your opponent's weapon away from you while circling your sword over and behind your head (Figure 6.80). While maintaining a check on the opponent's weapon hand, complete your sword's motion until it slashes the opponent's head or neck (Figure 6.81).

Figure 6.78

Figure 6.79

Figure 6.80

Figure 6.81

Sword and Dagger Application: Square off with your opponent in the abierta fighting stance (Figure 6.82). As the opponent initiates an overhead sword slash, simultaneously step to your right while intercepting the opponent's sword with the flat edge of your sword and checking/cutting his weapon hand with the dagger in your left hand (Figure 6.83). Immediately on impact, extend your dagger to move your opponent's weapon away from you while circling your sword over and behind your head (Figure 6.84). While maintaining a check on the opponent's weapon hand, complete your sword's motion until it slashes the opponent's head or neck (Figure 6.85).

Figure 6.82

Figure 6.83

Figure 6.84

Figure 6.85

CADENA REAL

Cadena real refers to a royal chain or necklace. The structure of the technique is one of meeting and redirecting an oncoming strike, then countering in one sweeping motion—much like tracing a necklace or chain around an opponent's neck. This technique is best used in close range and against downward horizontal or diagonal blows.

Stick Application: Square off with your opponent in the abierta fighting stance (Figure 6.86). As the opponent initiates an overhead stick strike, simultaneously step your left foot to the top-left corner of an inverted triangle while parrying the opponent's stick by raising your stick above your head and making contact with its tip on the tip of your opponent's stick (Figure 6.87). As the opponent's stick continues its motion, simultaneously use the forearm of your weapon arm and your left hand to redirect and check the opponent's arm while delivering a horizontal strike to his temple (Figure 6.88).

Figure 6.86

Figure 6.87

Figure 6.88

Sword Application: Square off with your opponent in the abierta fighting stance (Figure 6.89). As the opponent initiates an overhead sword slash, simultaneously step your left foot to the top-left corner of an inverted triangle while parrying the opponent's sword with the flat edge of your sword by raising your sword above your head (Figure 6.90). As the opponent's sword continues its motion, simultaneously use the forearm of your weapon arm and your left hand to redirect and check the opponent's arm, while delivering a horizontal slash to his neck (Figure 6.91).

Figure 6.89

Figure 6.90

Figure 6.91

Sword and Dagger Application: Square off with your opponent in the abierta fighting stance (Figure 6.92). As the opponent initiates an overhead sword slash, simultaneously step your left foot to the top-left corner of an inverted triangle while parrying the opponent's sword with the flat edge of your sword by raising your sword above your head (Figure 6.93). As the opponent's sword continues its motion, simultaneously thrust your dagger into his waist while using the forearm of your weapon arm to redirect and check the opponent's weapon arm and simultaneously delivering a horizontal slash to his neck (Figure 6.94).

Figure 6.92

Figure 6.93

Figure 6.94

A LA CONTRA SERRADA

A la contra serrada connotes going against a close-quarters attack. The structure of the technique finds the defender moving in close to the attacker and using his forearm against the attacker's forearm while grabbing hold of the attacker's weapon hand with his left hand. This technique requires precise timing and should only be used in close quarters and against horizontal blows.

Stick Application: Square off with your opponent in the abierta fighting stance (Figure 6.95). As the opponent initiates a forehand horizontal stick strike, begin to shift your body to the right and move your weapon toward the opponent (Figure 6.96). As the opponent's strike reaches its full extension, you should have twisted your body enough so that your chest is parallel to his weapon, which allows you to check his weapon forearm with your weapon forearm and the top of his weapon hand with your left hand while simultaneously striking his head with your stick (Figure 6.97).

Figure 6.95

Figure 6.96

Figure 6.97

Sword Application: Square off with your opponent in the abierta fighting stance (Figure 6.98). As the opponent initiates a forehand horizontal sword slash, begin to shift your body to the right and move your weapon toward the opponent (Figure 6.99). As the opponent's slash reaches its full extension, you should have twisted your body enough so that your chest is parallel to his weapon, which allows you to check his weapon forearm with your weapon forearm and the top of his weapon hand with your left hand while simultaneously slashing his throat with your sword (Figure 6.100).

Figure 6.98

Figure 6.99

Figure 6.100

Sword and Dagger Application: Square off with your opponent in the abierta fighting stance (Figure 6.101). As the opponent initiates a forehand horizontal sword slash, immediately shift your body to the right while simultaneously checking his weapon forearm with your weapon forearm and slashing his throat with your sword (Figure 6.102). As the opponent's slash reaches its full extension, you should be in such a position as to be able to thrust your dagger into his side without being struck with his sword in the process (Figure 6.103).

Figure 6.101

Figure 6.102

Figure 6.103

PAUYON

Pauyon refers to leading with force, or moving toward the direction of your opponent's strike. In executing this technique you must position yourself behind your opponent's strike and strike him twice before he is able to land even a single blow. The technique is best applied at medium range against a diagonal backhand strike, but, with an acute sense of timing and spatial relationships in relation to your opponent's strike, it can also be applied in close quarters.

Stick Application: Square off with your opponent in the abierta fighting stance (Figure 6.104). As the opponent initiates a diagonal backhand stick strike, you stand your ground until his weapon is about two-thirds of the way to its intended target (Figure 6.105). At this point, the opponent has fully committed to his strike, now allowing you to step safely to the right, twist your hips, and deliver a horizontal strike to his head (Figures 6.106 and 6.107). You then reposition yourself to face the opponent again, check his attacking arm with your left hand (Figure 6.108), and execute a downward strike to his head with your stick (Figure 6.109).

Figure 6.104

Figure 6.105

Figure 6.106

Figure 6.107

Figure 6.108

Figure 6.109

Sword Application: Square off with your opponent in the abierta fighting stance (Figure 6.110). As the opponent initiates a diagonal backhand sword slash, you stand your ground until his weapon is about two-thirds of the way to its intended target (Figure 6.111). At this point the opponent has fully committed to his strike, now allowing you to step safely to the right, twist your hips, and deliver a horizontal slash to his eyes or temples (Figures 6.112 and 6.113). You then reposition yourself to face the opponent again, check his attacking arm with your left hand (Figure 6.114), and execute a downward slash to his throat with your sword (Figure 6.115).

Figure 6.110

Figure 6.111

Figure 6.112

Figure 6.113

Figure 6.114

Figure 6.115

Sword and Dagger Application: Square off with your opponent in the abierta fighting stance (Figure 6.116). As the opponent initiates a diagonal backhand sword slash, you stand your ground until his weapon is about two-thirds the way to its intended target (Figure 6.117). At this point the opponent has fully committed to his strike, now allowing you to step safely to the right, twist your hips, and deliver a horizontal slash to his eyes or temples with your sword (Figures 6.118 and 6.119). Reposition yourself to face the opponent again and check/cut his attacking arm with the dagger in your left hand (Figure 6.120), finishing with a downward slash to his throat with your sword (Figure 6.121).

Figure 6.116

Figure 6.117

Figure 6.118

Figure 6.119

Figure 6.120

Figure 6.121

Abaniko

Abaniko means "fan" and refers to the structure of the technique, which is fan-like in its motion. While many systems use the abaniko technique along a horizontal plane, striking both sides of a single target, in kalis Ilustrisimo it is performed diagonally, from high to low or from low to high. If performed on the same plane, the technique is not only easier to block but also leaves your body vulnerable for too long a period—if even only for a few seconds. This technique can be applied against any type of strike, and while it is most effective in close quarters, it can also be effectively applied at medium range.

Stick Application: Square off with your opponent in the abierta fighting stance (Figure 6.122). As the opponent initiates a downward stick strike, step your left foot to the top-left point on an inverted triangle while simultaneously parrying his striking arm with your left hand and striking his stomach with your stick (Figure 6.123). Maintain control of his attacking arm and rotate your weapon arm diagonally up to the left (Figure 6.124), to strike his temple with your stick (Figure 6.125). While still maintaining your control of his weapon arm, rotate your weapon hand diagonally down to the right (Figure 6.126) and strike his stomach with your stick (Figure 6.127).

Figure 6.122

Figure 6.123

Figure 6.124

Figure 6.125

Figure 6.126

Figure 6.127

Sword Application: Square off with your opponent in the abierta fighting stance (Figure 6.128). As the opponent initiates a downward sword slash, step your left foot to the top-left point on an inverted triangle while simultaneously parrying his striking arm with your left hand and chopping his stomach with your sword (Figure 6.129). Maintain control of his weapon arm and rotate your weapon arm diagonally up to the left (Figure 6.130), to slash his eyes with your sword (Figure 6.131). While maintaining your control of his weapon arm, rotate your weapon hand diagonally down to the right (Figure 6.132) and chop his stomach with your sword (Figure 6.133).

Figure 6.128

Figure 6.129

Figure 6.130

Figure 6.131

Figure 6.132

Figure 6.133

Sword and Dagger Application: Square off with your opponent in the abierta fighting stance (Figure 6.134). As the opponent initiates a downward sword slash, step your left foot to the top-left point on the inverted triangle while simultaneously parrying/cutting his striking arm with the dagger in your left hand and chopping his stomach with your sword (Figure 6.135). Maintain control of his attacking arm and rotate your right arm diagonally up to the left (Figure 6.136) and simultaneously slash his eyes with your sword while thrusting your dagger into his midsection (Figure 6.137). While maintaining your control of his weapon arm, rotate your right hand diagonally down to the right (Figure 6.138) and chop his stomach with your sword while slicing his wrist with your dagger (Figure 6.139).

Figure 6.134

Figure 6.135

Figure 6.136

Figure 6.137

Figure 6.138

Figure 6.139

RECTA

Recta means "direct" or "straight" and this is one of the fastest and most economical defensive techniques found in kalis Ilustrisimo, because it employs neither a preparatory block, a deflection, nor a parry before the weapon hits its intended target. In essence, you move out of range of your opponent's strike, while striking directly down on his attacking weapon or weapon arm. The technique is equally effective in any combat range.

Stick Application: Square off with your opponent in the abierta fighting stance (Figure 6.140). As the opponent initiates a forehand stick strike, utilize the lutang footwork along a 45-degree angle to move out of range of his strike while simultaneously striking down on his forearm with your stick (Figure 6.141).

Figure 6.140

Figure 6.141

Sword Application: Square off with your opponent in the abierta fighting stance (Figure 6.142). As the opponent initiates a forehand sword slash, utilize the equis footwork to move out of range of his slash while simultaneously slashing diagonally across on his forearm with your sword (Figure 6.143).

Figure 6.142

Figure 6.143

Sword and Dagger Application: Square off with your opponent in the abierta fighting stance (Figure 6.144). As the opponent initiates a forehand sword slash, utilize the lutang footwork along a 45-degree angle to move out of range of his strike while simultaneously parrying his sword with your dagger and slashing diagonally across his forearm with your sword (Figure 6.145).

Figure 6.144

Figure 6.145

KABAY-AN

Kabay-an refers to riding a horse. In this technique, the motions of the arms moving from high to low to high resemble the arms of a horseman riding with reigns in hand. The technique is performed by moving off the line of attack and positioning your weapon on top of the opponent's to direct it downward, thus opening up his upper body to a counterattack. Be sure to drop your weight to the left when lowering your weapon, then uncoil it to the right while counterattacking. The technique is too slow for close quarters but is quite effective at both medium and long ranges.

Stick Application: Square off with your opponent in the abierta fighting stance (Figure 6.146). As the opponent initiates a forehand stick strike, maneuver to the right while simultaneously dropping your stick down on top of his and placing your left hand on top of your stick for support (Figure 6.147). Immediately on impact, forcefully direct your opponent's stick to the ground (Figure 6.148); using his resistance to rebound your stick, execute an upward diagonal strike to his chin (Figure 6.149).

Figure 6.146

Figure 6.147

Figure 6.148

Figure 6.149

Sword Application: Square off with your opponent in the abierta fighting stance (Figure 6.150). As the opponent initiates a forehand sword slash, maneuver to the right while simultaneously dropping the flat edge of your sword down on top of his and placing your left hand on the flat edge of your sword for support (Figure 6.151). Immediately on impact, forcefully direct your opponent's sword to the ground (Figure 6.152), using his resistance to rebound your sword to execute an upward diagonal slash to his throat (Figure 6.153).

Figure 6.150

Figure 6.151

Figure 6.152

Figure 6.153

Sword and Dagger Application: Square off with your opponent in the abierta fighting stance (Figure 6.154). As the opponent initiates a forehand sword slash, maneuver to the right while crossing your sword and dagger and simultaneously dropping the flat edges of both down on top of his sword (Figure 6.155). Immediately on impact, forcefully direct your opponent's sword to the ground (Figure 6.156), using his resistance to rebound your sword to execute an upward diagonal slash to his throat (Figure 6.157) followed by a dagger thrust to his heart (Figure 6.158).

Figure 6.154

Figure 6.155

Figure 6.156

Figure 6.157

Figure 6.158

Methods of Disarming

While techniques in disarming are plentiful, they are difficult to apply on an actively moving and fighting opponent. Therefore, in kalis Ilustrisimo they are considered secondary, or even tertiary, techniques. That is, they are techniques employed after an initial direct strike to the opponent or defensive maneuver has been executed, thus increasing their chances of success.

At long range, disarming is achieved by directly striking the weapon-holding hand or the weapon itself with great force. However, when at close or medium ranges and engaging an active opponent, you must first strike the opponent (perhaps several times) to divert his attention away from his weapon and then employ a joint lock to immobilize his weapon-holding arm in order to force him to release his weapon. You must also place yourself in such a position when disarming your opponent as to be out of the trajectory of any follow-up strike he might employ with his other hand (be it empty or also holding a weapon).

While there are no specific names to disarming techniques in kalis Ilustrisimo, they can be performed in several ways: by direct striking, by immobilizing the attacker's arm or wrist with your hand and releasing his weapon with your weapon, and by immobilizing his arm or wrist with your weapon and releasing the weapon with your hand. Moreover, at the completion of a disarming technique, you can either eject the opponent's weapon or retain it for your own follow-up use. Disarming can be done weapon against weapon or with empty hands against weapon.

The following are sample disarming techniques demonstrated as stick against stick, empty hands against knife, and handkerchief against knife. Experiment with using each method with and against a variety of weapons and strikes to see which work best in which scenarios. Moreover, when first learning these techniques, it is best for your partner to cooperate with you; after a period of time your partner should try his best to retain his weapon. It is only in this way that you will come to truly understand the true nature of the techniques.

STICK AGAINST STICK

Technique One

Face your opponent in the abierta guard (Figure 7.1). As he initiates a diagonal backhand strike to your knee (Figure 7.2), step your right foot to the right while striking your stick horizontally against his (Figure 7.3). Striking with force to the portion of your opponent's stick just above his thumb will force him to release his weapon (Figure 7.4).

Figure 7.1

Figure 7.2

Figure 7.3

Figure 7.4

Technique Two

Face your opponent in the abierta guard (Figure 7.5). As he initiates a horizontal backhand strike to your waist (Figure 7.6), utilize the lutang footwork to bring your lead leg back 90 degrees while shifting your body to the left and striking diagonally down on your opponent's wrist (Figure 7.7). The force of this blow will force your opponent to drop his weapon (Figure 7.8).

Figure 7.5

Figure 7.6

Figure 7.7

Figure 7.8

Technique Three

Face your opponent in the abierta guard position (Figure 7.9). As he initiates a diagonal forehand strike, defend (similar to estrella) by parrying his stick with your vertically held stick, while grabbing the section of his stick above his thumb with your left hand (Figure 7.10). As you continue the motion of your stick, unbalance your opponent by pulling his stick to your left (Figure 7.11), then continue your stick's motion until it strikes your opponent in the mid-section (Figure 7.12). From here, step your left foot up and in line with your opponent's lead foot while inserting your stick under and behind his weapon (Figure 7.13). By simultaneously striking down on his arm with the butt end of your stick and pulling his stick with your left hand, you will be able to force him to release his weapon (Figure 7.14).

Figure 7.9

Figure 7.10

Figure 7.11

Figure 7.12

Figure 7.13

Figure 7.14

Technique Four

Face your opponent in the abierta guard position (Figure 7.15). As he initiates a diagonal forehand strike, defend (similar to estrella) by parrying his stick with your vertically held stick while grabbing the section of his stick above his thumb with your left hand (Figure 7.16). While maintaining control of his weapon and keeping it at bay, execute a horizontal blow to the opponent's midsection (Figures 7.17 and 7.18) and then head or collarbone (Figure 7.19). While continuing your strike's motion, utilize the lutang footwork by sliding your right foot directly back while at the same time moving your opponent's weapon hand so that it is in front of your right side (Figure 7.20). Place your right foot in front again while lifting your opponent's weapon arm to unbalance him and placing the wrist or forearm of your weapon arm against the tip of his stick (Figure 7.21). Disarm the opponent by simultaneously twisting your hips to the left in tandem with your forearm and pulling back with your left hand (Figure 7.22).

Figure 7.15

Figure 7.16

Figure 7.17

Figure 7.18

Figure 7.19

Figure 7.20

Figure 7.21

Figure 7.22

Technique Five

Face your opponent in the abierta guard position (Figure 7.23). As he initiates a forehand high thrust, parry the tip of his stick down with your left hand while repositioning your stick so that it is parallel to the ground (Figure 7.24). As your opponent's thrust continues its motion, continue to simultaneously guide it down with your left hand and thrust your stick into his sternum while sliding your right leg back so as to allow the thrust to miss your body (Figure 7.25). In the same motion, circle your stick under (Figure 7.26) and to the outside of your opponent's weapon wrist while guiding his weapon forward with your left hand (Figure 7.27). It is the concurrent motion of pushing forward with your left hand and pulling your hips and stick back that will force him to release his weapon (Figure 7.28).

Figure 7.23

Figure 7.24

Figure 7.25

Figure 7.26

Figure 7.27

Figure 7.28

Technique Six

Face your opponent in the abierta guard position (Figure 7.29). As he initiates an upward diagonal strike, lower your stick (Figure 7.30), then simultaneously step forward with your left leg and place your left hand to the side of his stick and the base of your stick against the base of his stick (Figure 7.31). You will be able to disarm him by holding your stick in place as a fulcrum while pushing your left hand horizontally to the right (Figure 7.32).

Figure 7.29

Figure 7.30

Figure 7.31

Figure 7.32

Empty Hands Against Knife

Technique One

Face your opponent in a left-lead abierta guard position (Figure 7.33). As he initiates a high knife thrust, simultaneously take a step diagonally left to move off the line of attack and parry the knife down with the edge of your left hand along its flat edge, thrusting at his eyes with the fingers of your right hand (Figure 7.34). While the opponent is distracted, immediately snatch his wrist with your right hand to effect a wrist lock and pull him off balance by shifting your body weight to your right leg (Figures 7.35 and 7.36). As the opponent falls forward, shift your body weight forward again in an effort to thrust the knife into his midsection (Figure 7.37), and then disarm him by simultaneously lowering your right hand and raising your left hand (Figure 7.38). While maintaining a hold on the attacker's right wrist with your right hand, circle your left hand counterclockwise up (Figures 7.39 and 7.40), then drop it and your body weight down on his inner elbow (Figure 7.41). As the opponent falls forward, forcefully raise your body weight by standing, while taking control of his head with your left arm (Figure 7.42). You can then disable your opponent by locking his head with both hands and twisting it (Figures 7.43 and 7.44).

Figure 7.33

Figure 7.34

Figure 7.35

Figure 7.36

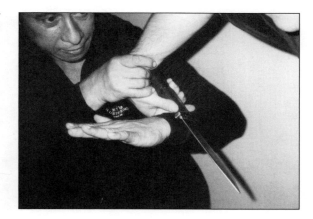

Figure 7.37

Figure 7.38

Figure 7.39

Figure 7.40

Figure 7.41

Figure 7.42

Figure 7.43

Figure 7.44

Technique Two

Face your opponent in the abierta guard position (Figure 7.45). As he initiates a high knife thrust, simultaneously step your right leg diagonally to the right and parry the inside of his weapon hand with your left hand, thrusting at his eyes with the fingers of your right hand (Figure 7.46). While the opponent is distracted, circle his weapon hand down and then up to the right with your left hand while sliding your right leg back to move you off the line of danger (Figures 7.47 and 7.48). To disarm your opponent, slide your right leg forward again while pushing your right forearm forward against the flat edge of the knife (Figures 7.49 and 7.50). While maintaining a secure hold on your opponent's right hand, encircle your right arm around it counterclockwise (Figures 7.51 and 7.52). This will force your opponent to turn his back, allowing you to concurrently lock his arm and neck (Figure 7.53).

Figure 7.45

Figure 7.46

Figure 7.47

Figure 7.48

Figure 7.49

Figure 7.50

Figure 7.51

Figure 7.52

Figure 7.53

Technique Three

Face your opponent in the abierta guard position (Figure 7.54). As he initiates a downward overhead thrust, intercept him and then grab the wrist of his weapon hand with your left hand, while thrusting at his eyes with the fingers of your right hand (Figure 7.55). While the opponent is distracted, twist his wrist to the left to immobilize his weapon arm (Figure 7.56) while circling your left arm counterclockwise down and then up to strike the side of his elbow (Figure 7.57). This will at once turn his back and bend his arm so that you can grab his throat with your left hand (Figure 7.58) and then pull his head back into the knife (Figure 7.59).

Figure 7.54

Figure 7.55

Figure 7.56

Figure 7.57

Figure 7.58

Figure 7.59

HANDKERCHIEF AGAINST KNIFE

As an example of how to disarm a knife with a flexible weapon, we have illustrated here the panyo, or handkerchief, technique. Since most people in the Philippines, and indeed around the world, carry such an innocent-looking piece of cloth, it is a natural weapon of defense.

To perform the disarm, face your opponent in a right lead stance while holding the handkerchief at its ends on an angle from your right hip to above your left hip (Figure 7.60). As he initiates a high knife thrust, step forward and up to the left while raising and positioning the cloth to the outside of his weapon (Figure 7.61). Once to the side of his weapon, redirect it by lowering your left wrist down on the flat edge of the knife (Figure 7.62), and then raising your right hand above his wrist (Figure 7.63). In the same motion, and while maintaining a check on the knife, cover his forearm with the cloth (Figure 7.64). Now pull your left hand back while pushing down on your opponent's arm with your right arm, thus locking it (Figure 7.65). You can then disarm the knife by simultaneously lowering your right hand, raising your left hand (Figure 7.66), then pulling the cloth ends in opposite directions (Figure 7.67).

Figure 7.60

Figure 7.61

Figure 7.62

Figure 7.63

Figure 7.64

Figure 7.65

Figure 7.66

Figure 7.67

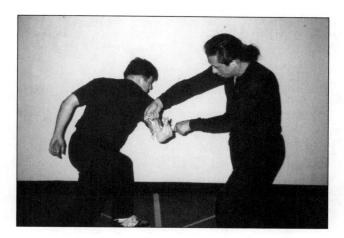

PART IV

The Combative Encounter

Combative
Sign Language

Since the Philippines is an archipelago that is home to several hundred ethnolinguistic groups, it is not surprising that its inhabitants have fought one
another since time immemorial. As the martial arts changed in focus over the
centuries from group to single combat, and since the practitioners of them did
not necessarily speak a common language, a method of communicating intentions should two warriors meet became necessary. This became even more
necessary in times of peace, when a practitioner of one system from one island
wished to practice with a practitioner of another system in another area. Since
spoken language was largely ineffective, sign language through a system of
body postures was developed over time to communicate practitioners' intentions. Thus, practitioners of different arnis and eskrima systems from different
ethnolinguistic groups were able to either practice together, have a friendly
test of skill, or engage in a fight to the death, knowing ahead of time what the
purpose of the encounter was.

DEMONSTRATION OR PRACTICE

When wishing to present yourself as a nonaggressive person, you would pose in one of two ways. If you were interested only in demonstrating your skills or in seeing the movements of another practitioner, you would first execute a series of movements representative of your style and then present yourself as inoffensive by separating your arms, palms up (Figure 8.1).

Figure 8.1

If you were interested in engaging another practitioner in training or give-and-take attack and defense training, you would point the tip of your weapon toward the forearm of your extended arm (Figure 8.2). As the weapon and arm did not touch, this symbolically represented keeping a safe distance between you and the other practitioner, thus indicating "play" or practice.

Figure 8.2

MATCHING SKILLS

Where sparring was concerned, if you were interested in engaging your opponent in light sparring, you would assume the above posture but touch the tip of your weapon against the skin of your forearm. However, if you were feeling a bit more adventurous and wanted to engage another practitioner in more serious, heavy-contact sparring, you would indicate this by either crossing your weapon over your forearm or crossing your extended forefinger across the tip of your weapon (Figure 8.3).

Figure 8.3

FIGHTING TO THE DEATH

And when the occasion arose that a death match was in hand, you would indicate this by pointing your weapon to the ground and the finger of your
extended arm to the sky. This indicated that one of you would remain on
Earth, while the other went to Heaven (or another place!) (Figure 8.4). Since
most death matches were carried out with bladed weapons, in such a case you
would extend the point of your sword to the ground, while extending the
point of your dagger to the sky (Figure 8.5).

Figure 8.4

Figure 8.5

CHAPTER NINE

Spiritual Fortitude

When engaging another eskrimador in a fight, you must possess the proper spiritual fortitude, or be centered and "at one" with yourself and your opponent. One is able to develop a high sense of self-esteem and confidence through daily training of techniques and a centered spirit through engaging in realistic drills and sparring sessions. While this is well enough for daily life and even general self-defense, in the Filipino view it is not enough for actual combative encounters with another practitioner.

Since pride and reputation are on the line, such encounters leave either one or both participants seriously injured or dead at the end of a few seconds. This thought alone is enough to break combatants' concentration and "spirit," if they have not had the opportunity to "test their skills" several times in the past. It is at this time that the eskrimador uses the power of prayer and the possession of amulets to invoke the spirits for divine intervention, assistance, and courage.

Anting-anting are amulets held on or in the body that possess the power of the spirit world and offer courage and protection to their bearer. Oracion are prayers or incantations, generally in an admixture of Latin and native Filipino dialects, that do much the same. The difference between them is that anting-anting are generally only able to protect the bearer or give him courage, while oracion can do that in addition to weakening the opponent, breaking his fighting spirit, or forcing him to drop his weapon.

Antonio Ilustrisimo was a staunch believer in such things and possessed both. Regarding such things, Good Friday is the solemn day for arnisadors who are masters of oracion, that is, those who are able to control the spirit world through their charms and prayers. It is on this day that they test whether they still have their power, or whether they have lost it.

Every year on Good Friday, Tatang would wander to a deserted field followed by both believers and skeptics. He would prop up pieces of paper on which he had written incantations. He would then invite anyone with a gun (and many people carry them in the Philippines) to shoot at the paper at point-blank range. Amazingly, no one ever succeeded in hitting the target with their bullets, despite the barrel of their gun touching it.

When one of the shooters was asked what he felt when shooting at the paper, he replied, "Nothing extraordinary happens while one is aiming at the paper. But the moment one pulls the trigger, an invisible force tugs the barrel of the gun aside and makes one miss. Sometimes the gun would refuse to fire altogether." If oracion can keep bullets from hitting their intended target, even a sharp blade poses no real threat to the eskrimador who possesses them.

Antonio Ilustrisimo would go home to recite his oracion twice a day at specified times—every day without fail. He also had his anting-anting tattooed on his chest so that it would forever be a part of him. During his fights, he would mentally recite his oracion. Given that he never lost a match—friendly or to the death—one has a difficult time just dismissing such things. As a testament to his uncanny powers, Antonio Diego is also a true believer and possessor of both anting-anting and oracion, and has also not lost a match.

CHAPTER TEN

Fighting Principles and Strategies

Divine intervention aside, in order to use your art effectively you must know how and when to apply your skills properly. The kalis Ilustrisimo system is a fighting art whose techniques are based on a solid foundation of principles and strategies realized by the late grandmaster Antonio Ilustrisimo. It was over an eighty-year period of evaluation and analysis, and as a result of his numerous combative encounters with live blades, that he realized the importance of the fundamental principles and strategies underlying his style of swordplay.

You must be sure not to mistake fighting principles and strategies for the techniques themselves. They are not. Rather, they are what make the techniques effective. The following is a discussion of the intellectual framework of kalis Ilustrisimo.

KEEP CALM AND RELAXED

You may feel that you are strong when you are tense, but that is an illusion. In reality, you are pitting one muscle against another and subtracting from the net force you could exert. Your speed is also impaired when you're tense because the contracting muscles have to overcome the force of the tensed antagonistic muscles. Thus, you cannot keep calm without relaxing, and you cannot relax without first becoming calm; the two go hand in hand.

It is not easy for one to relax when learning a new technique or when sparring for the first time. But that's okay. With more experience, you should grow more calm and relaxed. A good conscience helps.

KNOW YOUR DISTANCE

As discussed earlier, there are three basic fighting ranges in kalis Ilustrisimo: short range, middle range, and long range. Which range you are fighting in depends upon your reach, the reach of your opponent, and the relative size of both of your weapons. If you have a shorter reach, you would have a shorter fighting distance compared to your opponent. Thus, you and your opponent should have different fighting distances.

Knowing what range you are in, what techniques you can effectively apply while in it, and how to effectively maneuver between ranges is of utmost importance when attempting to position yourself in a more advantageous position than your opponent.

MOVE WITHOUT DELAY

Always remain relaxed and strike directly and without delay. While in the classical styles of arnis, the arnisador brings his weapon way back before striking, in real combat, there should be no delay in movement, only reaction and forward movement. In contrast to the classical style, the kalis Ilustrisimo practitioner counters as soon as his weapon clears the tip of his opponent's weapon.

This is why the fighting guard stance is such that the weapon is held up and only slightly back. The weapon of the kalis Ilustrisimo practitioner travels less distance and with less telegraphing of intention than does the traditional arnisador, thus making him harder to block and counter.

Use the Shortest Path for Your Trajectory

To be twice as speedy as your opponent, you do not have to be born twice as fast. You only have to halve the distance your blow travels. This means: keep it short and simple. After all, it's not how fast a strike travels but how soon it gets there that counts, and timing plays an important role in this.

To halve the distance and thus shorten the striking time: always keep your weapon between yourself and your opponent; strike from where your weapon is; do not draw it back in an attempt to generate momentum.

Conversely, if your opponent draws back his weapon to gain momentum, strike the moment his weapon retracts. He will be caught with his weapon going in the wrong direction and thus unable to counter yours effectively.

Finally, eschew complicated maneuvers and techniques. They may look brilliant, and they may be rapidly executed, but they take too much time to execute and are therefore inefficient.

Use the Weight of Your Body

A physical law states that force equals mass times momentum. Thus, the force generated by the mass of your body is many times greater than that generated by the mass of your arms. Therefore, lower your body weight as you deliver downward blows, rock it forward behind your thrusting techniques, rock it backward on your pulling techniques, and twist your waist as you deliver circular blows.

However, be sure not to overdo it, as you may be thrown off balance in the process, or your movements may become wide and cumbersome.

The secret is to learn how to modulate the use of your weight. There are times when you should only use a fraction of your body weight, times when you should use a little more, and times when you should use your full weight to deliver a finishing blow.

GUIDE THE OPPONENT'S FORCE

In some instances, it is more difficult for a strong man to learn arnis, because he relies on his strength to overpower his opponent. But what if he meets a more powerful man one day? Then his strength is useless.

It is with this in mind that you should not meet your opponent's force head on, his blow directly. Rather, learn how to apply force at an angle to the direction your opponent is executing power so you can guide his force and dissolve it.

KNOW WHEN TO BREAK THE RULES

Rules are made to fit the general case. However, in combat, there are no general cases.

Scientists at first believed gravity to be universal. Now it turns out that there are antigravity particles.

The only safe rule about human beings is that they are full of surprises. When surprises happen, be prepared to break the existing rules and make new rules of your own as you go. This way you will never be caught off guard.

MOVE IN EVERY DIRECTION

The strategy of stepping in all eight directions *(walong apak)* is used when facing multiple opponents. Imagine yourself standing in the middle of a circle that has been divided by lines along the eight primary directions. To engage the multiple opponents who have surrounded you, you plant one foot at the center of the circle while stepping with the other to the various eight direc-tions in an effort to strike one, then another, opponent and maneuver out of harm's way.

FLANK THE BLIND SIDE

As described earlier, the movements of flanking an opponent are called combate heneral, wherein the defender moves in the same direction as the opponent's blow, and trunkada heneral, wherein the defender moves in the direction in which the blow was initiated. They are strategies for flanking your opponent to his side. With this, you are able to move off his line of attack, face him at a 90-degree angle to his blind side, and effectively land your counterattack.

CREATE OPENINGS

The ability to draw or force your opponent to commit to a technique is known as *enganyo,* or feinting, of which there are twelve basic methods in kalis Ilustrisimo. Feints are most effectively employed when taking the offensive but are also effective when countering an opponent who has previously been able to block your counters. In essence, you feint a first blow, and while the oppo-nent responds to it, you follow up with the intended blow to the openings on his body you have created.

USE BROKEN RHYTHM

The use of broken rhythm, or unusual timing in strikes and steps, is one of the primary strategies applied in kalis Ilustrisimo. In essence, you want your tech-niques to "fall between the cracks" of your opponent's, thus enabling you to strike him before his blows have reached their destination. Moreover, by using broken rhythm in conjunction with feinting, you are able to "throw off" your opponent's timing and control the encounter.

Afterword

We hope that you have found this first book on kalis Ilustrisimo interesting, informative, and composed of techniques and strategies that you can use. Keep in mind, while training, that exaggerated and flowery movements and techniques that require extreme flexibility and speed have no place in real combat, only in showmanship. Thus, when using your art for fighting, as opposed to physical fitness or as a hobby, it is best to be simple and direct. Stick to the basics, as these are at once the foundation, nucleus, and advanced techniques of the art.

With regard to arnis as a sport, we must never lose sight of the fact that eskrima and arnis are combat arts. However, to draw crowds and increase the popularity of the Filipino martial arts, they need to be developed as sport. Regardless, do not sacrifice realistic fighting methods for sport training, sport target selection, and sport rules. These only work when wearing the full body armor that we see in today's tournaments. Among true eskrimadors, no armor is, or has ever been, worn when testing one's skills. And while this may not be the popular way to go today, if all that is used in tournaments is padded sticks, and maybe hand and eye protection, the art will not totally degenerate along the lines of many of the so-called modern martial arts.

We should also never forget that we are simulating a battle in the sport arena, not determining who has the most number of points. For in actual combat, any one of those points could have ended the fight. One must realize that the one with the most number of points could rightfully have been killed with the first blow of the participant with the least number of points.

With this in mind, in order to keep arnis realistic, even when engaging it as sport, we have to devise rules that are not a mockery of reality. We should never forget that we are practicing and learning combat arts, not playing Nintendo.

Let those who insist on and believe in victory by points go to video arcades. Those who want to learn and experience the true art of arnis are always welcome in our open-air training and sparring sessions in Luneta Park or our clubs throughout the Philippines and around the world.

On another note, regardless of the respect in which you hold your teacher, don't blindly follow him. The system is always more important than the man, so you must learn your limitations as well as your abilities. Certain techniques and styles demand certain physical attributes, often similar to those of the person who created the system. Let's say a small, diminutive master is the mentor of a big, hulking man. Doesn't the big man look awkward and clumsy trying to do the techniques of the small master? That's because the small master's techniques were taking advantage of his small size and speed. And while the big man may eventually learn and master the small master's system, he will have sacrificed the advantage of his size, weight, and stability for a style meant for the exact opposite of his physical attributes. So be critical of your training, understanding your art's inherent concepts and principles as they can be applied to your individual build, height, and mentality.

Afterword

In closing, we would like to suggest that we all try to become good people in the course of our lives, help others as much as possible, and avoid all unnecessary fights. If you are forced to fight, you will be more relaxed if you enter a fight with a clear conscience. And while the good may not always win, they face death more calmly.

The Lineage of Kalis Ilustrisimo

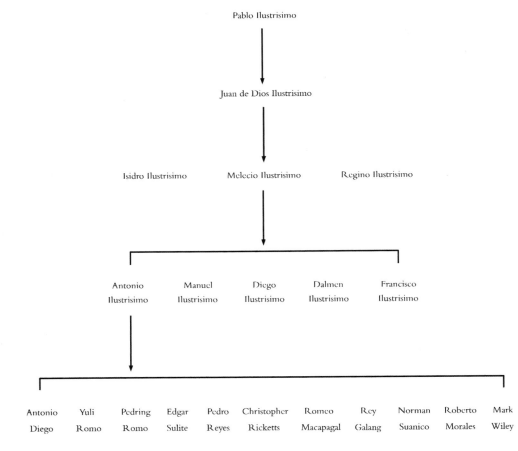

Pablo Ilustrisimo

Juan de Dios Ilustrisimo

Isidro Ilustrisimo   Melecio Ilustrisimo   Regino Ilustrisimo

Antonio Ilustrisimo   Manuel Ilustrisimo   Diego Ilustrisimo   Dalmen Ilustrisimo   Francisco Ilustrisimo

Antonio Diego   Yuli Romo   Pedring Romo   Edgar Sulite   Pedro Reyes   Christopher Ricketts   Romeo Macapagal   Rey Galang   Norman Suanico   Roberto Morales   Mark Wiley

Active Practitioners of Kalis Ilustrisimo

Thomas Dy Tang	Miguel Zubiri	Ramon Tulfo	David Chan	Atty. Valdellon	Atty. Llariza
Hans Tan	Achie Sadaya	Nick Mustard	Nick Maaghop	Eddie Benin	Rolly Tadepa
Jessen Sta. Maria	Jun Pueblos	Jun Catilan	Benny Litonjua	Dodong Sta. Iglesia	Raul Guerrero

Glossary

A la contra cerrada—against close range

Abaniko—fan

Aldabis—upward diagonal strikes

Anting-anting—amulet

Bagsak—(1) dropping strike; (2) to drop; in this case, a sudden, forceful downward cut at a horizontally directed attack

Banda y banda—side to side striking

Boca de lobo—mouth of the wolf

Cadena real—a royal or real chain

Combate heneral—general combat concept of flanking

Cruzada—cross

De cadena—a series repetitive strikes

De campo—an open field or wide area, thus long range.

De elastiko—elastic

Doble carera—double race, or double route or path, as in both hands are running after each other while attacking.

Doblete—double

Equis—X-step or cross-legged

Estrella—star, as in stellar; here it denotes the starlike configuration of two crossed weapons

Florete—a fencing foil

Fraile—friar

Kabay-an—ride a horse

Lutang—to float; in this case, a type of backward footwork (*riterada*) that does not touch the ground as it moves backward and then forward again

Media Fraile—semi-friar

Oracion—a prayer or incantation

Pauyon—leading with the force, going with the force

Planchada—a flat plank or surface, a horizontal slicing

Pluma—pen

Praksion—fraction

Recta—direct or straight

Riterada—retreating

Rompida—up and down

Serrada—close-range or closed-guard or close-quarters technique

Sonkite—thrust and then strike combination

Sunod sampal—horizontal side-to-side swing

Tatlong bao—three shells

Tindig abierta—open fighting guard

Tindig serrada—closed fighting guard

Tusuk—thrust

Vertical—vertical block

Walong apak—eight steps

Further Reading

Galang, Reynaldo S. (1997, Sept.). The Fighting Arts of Bakbakan
International. *Martial Arts Legends Presents: Exotic Martial Arts,* pp. 8–13.

Inosanto, D. and Johnson, G. (1978). *The Filipino Martial Arts.* Los Angeles:
Know Now Publications.

Marasigan, Vicente. (1985). *A Banahaw Guru: Symbolic Deeds of Agapito
Illustrisimo.* Quezon City, Philippines: Ateneo de Manila University Press.

Reyes, Pedro. (1998). Filipino Martial Tradition, *RAPID Journal,* pp. 18–21.

Reyes, Pedro. (1999). Arnis and the Laws of Physics, *RAPID Journal,*
pp. 23–25.

Seibert, Gunner. (1995). *Arnis Eskrima Kali.* Berlin, Germany: Verlag Weinman.

Sulite, Edgar G. (1986). *The Secrets of Arnis.* San Juan, Philippines:
Socorro Books.

Sulite, Edgar G. (1993). *The Masters of Arnis, Kali and Eskrima.* San Juan,
Philippines: Socorro Books.

Wiley, Mark V. (1997). *Filipino Martial Culture.* Boston, MA: Charles E. Tuttle Co.

Wiley, Mark V. (1998). Fighting Strategy and Techniques of Kalis Ilustrisimo. *Karate International,* pp. 32–33.

Wiley, Mark V. (2001). *Filipino Fighting Arts: Theory and Practice.* Burbank, CA: Unique Publications.